God Bless you

Pastor R. B. McCartney

Revival Of Those Left Behind

by
Pastor R.B. McCartney

Bloomington, IN  Milton Keynes, UK

AuthorHouse™
1663 Liberty Drive,
Suite 200
Bloomington, IN 47403
www.authorhouse.com
Phone: 1-800-839-8640

AuthorHouse™ UK Ltd.
500 Avebury Boulevard
Central Milton
Keynes, MK9 2BE
www.authorhouse.co.uk
Phone: 08001974150

© 2007 Pastor R.B. McCartney. All rights reserved.

No part of this book may be reproduced, stored in a retrieval system, or transmitted by any means without the written permission of the author.

First published by AuthorHouse 1/15/2007

ISBN: 978-1-4259-8798-5 (sc)

Printed in the United States of America
Bloomington, Indiana

This book is printed on acid-free paper.

PREFACE

It is my belief God gave me the inspiration to write this book. I believe the Lord's return is near, and He is coming for a church which is ready and waiting for His return. If this book helps anyone avoid being left behind, or if you read it after the coming of Christ and repent of your sins I will have reached my goal for writing the book.

If you have lost loved ones I urge you to place this book in a place where it will be easy for them to find in case you are caught out in the rapture, and they are left behind.

This book is part fiction and the names used in it are fictitious, but we believe the things taking place after the rapture of the church will really take place similar to what is described in this book. Although the names and events are fictitious in this book, the Bible passages which are given and explained are not. All passages from the Bible are from the King James Version.

The book is about a great revival taking place on the earth of those who's loved ones have disappeared in the rapture. They are now ready to repent and serve Jesus at all cost.

I want to thank my wife Thelma of 55 years, for encouraging me in the writing of this book, and correcting my mistakes.

Many thanks to my friend Pastor Albert Warren for his time and the help he has given me getting this book ready to be published.

Chapter 1

WHERE IS EVERYONE

It was early in the morning when Josie awoke to sirens all over the city. She jumps out of bed wondering what is going on so early in the morning. There must be a really bad fire, or a bad accident somewhere. She runs over to the window and looks out. A car has run up on the curb and into the neighbor's tree. The neighbors were out looking at the car. She calls for her husband Stan, but he is in the shower and doesn't hear her. She decided she would go into the children's room and check on them. To her surprise their beds were empty. She pulled back the cover to find their night clothes were still in the bed. She thought they had probably gotten dressed and gone down to the kitchen. She checked in the closet. Their clothes she had told them to put on before they had retired for the night were still hanging in the closet. She thought this is really strange; they wouldn't go around in the nude. She runs down to the kitchen to find they are not there. She goes to every room, but they are nowhere to be found. She begins to panic, and begins to scream to the top of her voice, "Stan! Stan! The kids are missing! Oh God please helps us! Where could they be?"

By this time Stan begins to be concerned. He said to Josie. "Now just calm down. I am sure the children are here somewhere. Just get hold of yourself; we will find them." He begins to go to every room calling for the children. "Maybe they are hiding," he said. He begins to look for them in all the closets, and under the beds, but they are not to be found.

"Do you think someone has kidnapped the kids," said Josie? "Or maybe some aliens from outer space have taken them, let's call the police,"

"No wait" said Stan, "I will go outside and see if I can find them."

"Ok" said Josie, "while you look outside I am going to call over to Bud and Maria' house, they may have gone over there since they only live a block away, but I doubt if they would go anywhere without their clothes."

Stan runs outside to look for the children. When he gets outside he finds that people all up and down the street are weeping and wailing looking for their family. They are all asking the same question, have you seen my children, have you seen my wife, have you seen my husband, have you seen my mother or father. The answer to everyone is no! Stan walks over to the wrecked car. A few people are standing around. Stan asks, "Was anyone hurt?"

One guy said, "We don't know, there isn't anyone in the car, but there is clothing lying in the seat as if someone had just vanished out of them. There is a car seat in the back with baby clothes in it, but no baby."

By this time Josie has come out of the house, she said to Stan, "I tried to call Maria, their answering machine came on, but I couldn't get anyone to pickup. I tried them several times but they wouldn't pick up. Let's go call the police," said Josie, "maybe they will know something."

"Good luck", said one of the neighbors, "I have tried to call them several times, but the circuits are all busy."

By this time someone has identified the wrecked car. Someone said it is the family living next door to him. He said, "They were real religious, in fact we had thought they might be a little too religious, all they wanted to talk about was Jesus. They never would miss a service at their church. They were always trying to convert other people. They were really good neighbors, if you had a need they were always there for you. They had made mention they were going to some kind of church meeting today and was leaving early this morning. There doesn't seem to be anyone at their home, I have no idea what has happened to them, but I do know they had mentioned something about Jesus coming for the church. I don't know, it's a crazy idea, but something has sure taken place and I don't know what."

Josie said to Stan, "I have an idea, let's go down to Bud and Maria's and see if they are home. They were very religious, let's check on them."

Bud and Maria only lived a block away so they had opted to walk down. When they arrived at their house both of their cars were home. "They must be home," said Josie. They rang the door bell, knocked on the door, called out for them with a loud voice, going all around the house knocking and calling to no avail.

"I am determined," said Josie, "they have gone in the rapture of the church. Maria used to tell me about it. She said Jesus was going to come as a thief in the night for all of those that would be looking for his coming. I really believe it has happened."

"Well I am not too sure," said Stan. "Let's go back home and see what the news is saying."

When they arrived back home and turned on the TV. Set. The news reporters were talking about how much problem they had trying to get the news on the air. They said, "Very few people have showed up for work. Some of them couldn't be reached by phone, e mail, or fax. Some had arrived for work only to leave again when they had gotten a call or e mail to say some of their family was missing. Everything is in chaos here at the station. Just be patient with us and we will try to do our best and get the news out to you as soon as we can. We do know something serious has happened. There are people missing everywhere. Nobody knows just yet what has really happened. Some are saying terrorist is behind it, others are saying aliens from another planet are responsible. None of this seems to make sense.

There have been planes to go down all over the world, big rigs, buses, and cars have crashed everywhere because the pilots and drivers are missing. This has caused other cars, busses; and trucks to crash. Subways in some of the major cities have been reported in a mess, with many accidents.

There aren't enough paramedics to take care of all the wounded people. The emergency rooms are packed, with people waiting in line for medical attention. Someone has mentioned a rapture of the church. We don't know what they are talking about, but as soon as we find out more we will let you know. We have been trying to reach some of the pastors of our churches to see if they know anything about a rapture of the church. Those we have been able to reach say they don't know anything about the rapture of the church. They say they haven't studied bible prophecy, but the bible doesn't mention the word rapture. There are some preachers in our town that do preach bible prophesies, but they don't answer their phones. We have left messages, but they haven't called us back.

We have tried reaching the governor of our state but all the lines are busy going into his office. We also have been trying to reach someone in Washington D.C. We were able to reach one of the President's aides. He said no one had seen the President this morning. They have been calling his office but have been unable to reach him. They are reporting to us that everything in Washington is in a chaotic state. Many key personnel are absent from their post.

Some of the airport controllers are missing from their post, resulting in planes in the air being unable to get down. Some are reporting they are getting low on fuel. In the air it looks like every one must watch out for him self, they are having near collisions because so many planes are coming in and not being able to land. There is one good thing; no planes are taking off at this time. Several planes have already crashed taking off or landing, some planes have just fallen from midair.

The armed forces are also in chaos their planes are also falling out of the air, some have crashed while landing. Ships are running into each other as if they are out of control. Smoke and fire is everywhere it is unbelievable. We are under attack from someone and we seem to be in a state of confusion. We haven't been able to determine if terrorist is involved or not. The reports coming in from over seas are not good. We will let you know as soon as something else develops."

You have just heard from Washington. Now we have our governor on the line let's go to her at this time. Governor we are glad you took the time out to talk with us, everyone wants to know what is going on we sure hope you can tell us. "Ok, thanks I will tell you what I know, and that is very little. We don't know just yet what is going on. We have been trying to call in the National Guard because we are in a state of emergency. Some of them don't answer their phone, and those that do are refusing to come in because they have someone in their family that is missing and they are looking for them.

We have been trying to call in the highway patrol, but can get only a few of them to come in. They are also reporting problems. Reports are coming in from the patrols out on the highways saying the roads are littered with wrecked cars and trucks. Many people are wounded or dead. Some of our patrol cars have been involved. One officer has said he has never seen the highways as littered with accidents as they are today. We also have reports of our airports being in a state of chaos. I am, going to be real honest with you, I don't know what is going on but as soon as I know I will let you know. I suggest you go to your churches. Church pastors are trained to help you in times like these.

That's a good idea said Josie to Stan, "lets go down to our Church, Pastor Joe will probably know something. He usually has an answer for everything."

Chapter 2

LADOCI CHURCH

Stan and Josie arrive at the church. The parking lot is almost full. "Wow!" Said Josie! "I don't think I ever saw this many cars at our church through the week." When they go inside the church, the church is packed with people weeping for their loved ones who are missing. One of the ushers tells Stan and Maria to have a seat, and tells them their pastor will be addressing the church soon. He is in his office studying the Word, and praying.

'This is strange," said Stan; "I don't see any small children any where in the church. People are praying, and asking God what has happened to their love ones. Some of them seem to be angry with God."

The song director decides maybe if they sing some courses it will change the mood of the people. It seems like everyone is at a funeral they are so sad. The pianist comes to the piano the song director begins to sing, but no one seems to want to help him. Finally in disgust he goes over and sets down with out another word.

Everyone begins to get very anxious for the pastor to come out. Some of the folks seem to really be getting upset. It seems like we have been waiting for hours. It looks like he is not going to show said one of the members. Why doesn't he come out and address us on this issue? One of the ushers goes to his office to check on him. The usher comes back to the podium and said, "Pastor Joe said to have patience; he will be out as soon as he can get things figured out."

One guy yells out, "What does he mean patience! We have been waiting a long time, my wife is missing and I think he knows where she is. If he doesn't come out soon I am going looking for him!"

Finally the pastor comes out of his office. By this time the church is packed with people standing up in the back. Pastor Joe takes his place at the podium; he is not in a joking mood as usual. In fact he doesn't even tell a joke. It had been his policy to tell a funny joke to begin his part of the service, but not today he is very solemn. He begins to speak, and begin to say, "I don't know what has happened. My wife and I also have some of our family missing. My wife's mother who lives in the parsonage with us is missing. Our daughter who lives close by has come over and said our grandchildren are missing. We haven't been able to reach our son, and daughter-in-law who live in another state, we don't know about them and their three children. We have also tried to reach my parents who live in another state to no avail. My wife, daughter and son in law are over in the parsonage. My wife, and daughter are about to have a nervous breakdown. My son-in-law is trying to comfort them. I should be over there with them, but I felt my duty to you and I am here. I hope you appreciate me doing this for you. I have been praying, and studying the Bible this morning for answers. I don't know why but God seems to be far away.

The news people have said something about a rapture of the church where Jesus comes to take the church away as a thief. I have been studying this morning trying to find something on rapture, but it just isn't in the Bible. I can assure you the church is not gone, we are still here, if the church was gone to heaven we would be in heaven, we wouldn't be here this morning. I can assure you Jesus will not leave one church member behind. God is a God of love.

Some of these radical preachers have been preaching grace with works. It doesn't make any difference how you live, as long as you confess Jesus as the son of God. We can live however we please; it isn't any body's business but our own. My wife and I like to party, and have a little fun. We love going to places like Las Vegas, gamble, have a few drinks, watch the girlie shows, and comedy shows. We hear a lot of good jokes there. Of course some of the jokes are a little off color, I can't tell them from the pulpit. This is just the human side of us all. I don't see anything wrong with these things, and I sure wouldn't teach you any different. Everyone sins a little every day.

I know that some of the older more conservative people like my mother-in-law, and my parents have felt different. They were all pretty radical when it came to serving Jesus. You might say they had a little of the Pharisee religion in them. Now don't get me wrong they were good people, and lived good lives, they grew up in a different world than the one I grew up in. Today we are living in a modern world. We have TV, Computers, cell phones, video games, fast cars, pornography, and several other things that they didn't have when they were growing up.

I heard one of those old time preachers preaching the other day; he was saying television had gotten so bad we shouldn't watch it. He also said computers were of the devil. I couldn't believe he would say computers were bad. He talked about the sex, violence, and bad language on television. He said young girls and boys were getting in trouble meeting different people on the internet. He said young men were being corrupted by nudity on TV and on the computer. He also talked about gays and lesbians. He said what they are doing is an abomination to God. He said he believes God is getting ready to judge this world. He said God is against homosexuality and lesbianism, fornication, sex out of wedlock, lying cheating, stealing, disobeying parents and other things. He really did beat up on the homosexuals, and lesbians. I thought who does he think he is? Where did he come from? Did he come from the dark ages? Doesn't he know homosexuals and lesbians were born that way? Doesn't he know we are in the 21st century? I thought about calling him up and set him straight. If I was attending his church and he were to preach things like he was preaching I would get up in the service and tell the people he was preaching lies. Then I would walk out.

Now to get back to what has just taken place today. I can assure you it is not the Lord coming back for his believers. The apostle Paul has said in, [II Thessalonians] 'that day will not come except there come a great falling away first and that man of sin be revealed". You don't see this happening do you? It is possible that terrorist is behind what is going on, or it is possible it could be someone from another planet, it could be brought on by the devil, but I don't really think so. The devil gets blamed for a lot of things that he doesn't do. I am sure before this day is over we will know what is happening, and our loved ones will be back with us, go to your homes, don't worry, I am sure the secret service is already working on the problem. Watch your televisions; I am sure the President will be explaining soon what is going on. I am sure everything is going to be ok." He goes into his office without another word.

The people are very unhappy with him. They feel he has really let them down. Every one seems to be in a very unhappy mood.

Stan and Josie talk to some of the people. One lady said, "I thought sure Pastor Joe would know what is going on. He has always had an answer for everything. I have always thought he was the smartest pastor in town. I am sure he will have an answer soon, and will address us again."

Josie said, "Yes, I was disappointed in Pastor Joe this morning. I had been told by a friend that he wasn't preaching the gospel, but she was attending a conservative church, they taught Christian's should be different from the world. They taught against gambling, drinking, and going to worldly places where people were doing sinful things. She would really irritate me sometimes."

A man speaks up and said, "I have always thought Pastor Joe was a way out in left field, but I liked going to church here. I have always been a party animal, I liked to hang out at bars and go to places where they had dancing girls. My wife would never go to those places. I tried to convince her it was ok, and then I would come with her to church. Sometimes my conscience would tell me these things were wrong, but I never heard Pastor Joe preach one word against the things I was doing. I had a friend at work which was always bugging me and telling me the rapture was going to take place, and I would get left behind but I would tell him salvation didn't have anything to do with works. I believe today he might have known some things I didn't know. When I got up this morning, and my wife and children were missing. I begin to think about what my friend had been telling me about a rapture of the church. Of course I knew Pastor Joe had said rapture was not in the Bible. I looked rapture up in the dictionary and the definition was caught up. When some of the people talk about it they are talking about Jesus coming for the church. When my wife and children were missing I begin to give this rapture business a thought and have decided it may have happened, Jesus may have come back for the church and our love ones are gone to be with Him."

After other people share their thoughts, Stan said, "Josie I think it is time we should be going, I don't think we will get any answers here today."

Josie said, "Ok" and they leave.

Chapter 3

AGAPE CHURCH

Stan and Maria were very disappointed in their pastor because he didn't have any answers. "I have a suggestion," said Josie, "let's go over to the church where Bud and Maria attend. Their pastor might have some answers." When they pulled into the parking lot, there was a few cars, but nothing like over at their church. When they walked into the church several people were down front praying. They were pleading with God to forgive them for not giving more attention to what their pastor had been preaching. One lady was asking God to forgive her of her sins and to receive her. She was telling God how wrong she had been. Her sister had tried to get her to accept Christ, and attend church. She had told her sister she was young, and had a lot of living to do. She had told her sister, when I am older I will serve Jesus. She was telling Jesus that she believed in him, but hadn't been ready to settle down.

There was this guy who had awakened in the morning to find his wife and children gone. He was telling God how his wife and children had tried to get him to attend church and accept Christ. He would tell his wife he wasn't ready then, but would make that decision later. He was telling the Lord how sorry he was that he had waited too late. He said, "I thought I loved my wife' and family but I guess I loved drinking and partying more. I was spending our hard earned money on drinking. I know they spent many nights wandering if I would be home that night. I can remember those Christmases that they didn't even have a decent meal, not to mention gifts. Oh God how wrong I have been, please forgive me for my sins and God if my wife and children are there with you today, please tell them I am sorry for the way I treated them."

Josie said to Stan, "look over to the right of the altar there is someone we know. It is Maria's sister Mary and her husband Bill, they know us maybe they can tell us what has happened." Stan and Josie move over to that side of the altar. Mary looks up and recognizes Stan and Josie. She said, "Look Bill it is Maria and Bud's friends." Mary and Bill grab Stan and Josie and begin to hug them; they begin to share with each other what has taken place. "What are you guys doing here," said Mary, "I thought you guys went to church over at the Ladoci church."

"We do," said Josie, "but our pastor doesn't seem to know what has happened. We thought maybe the pastor here would know something. Where is your pastor?" "He is not here," said Mary, "he is missing like my sister, her husband, and children, our children, our parents, and a lot of others we know. My sister tried to tell Bill and I we should start living for the Lord, and that the Lord would be coming soon. We would attend church on special occasions, we even went to the altar and prayed with the pastor once, but we weren't really sincere. I think we only went forward because Maria was bugging us. After that we would tell her we were Christians, but we didn't think we had to go to church all time. We knew that we weren't living for Christ. Maria and Bill would pick up our children, and take them to church.

Revival Of Those Left Behind

Our older son, who is in his teens now, finally quit going to church because we didn't go. Sometimes we would let him drink beer with us. We thought it wouldn't hurt anything, but now he is on drugs really bad and we don't even know where he is. We had heard the pastor say that prophecy was being fulfilled, and Jesus was coming soon. We didn't doubt him, but we thought we had plenty of time.

We know now that we have waited too long. Jesus has come, our children and loved ones are gone to heaven, and we have been left behind. We don't know much about it, but the pastor had said some people that hadn't been saved, and some that were not looking for him at his coming would be left behind, but they would turn to him after the rapture. They would make it to heaven, but they would have to go into the great tribulation period. We are determined we want to go to heaven with our friends and family. So what ever it takes we are determined to make it. We would like to find someone that knows their Bible to lead us in a Bible study to find out just what we need to do."

A guy was praying nearby. He overheard their conversation. He said; "maybe I can lead a Bible study. I have been a deacon in this church for 15 years. I have studied the Bible; I know the Bible very well. I never missed a service at our church. The pastor and I were best friends. I loved his preaching, and because I studied the word, I knew he always preached the truth. When I awoke this morning to sirens, and found my wife and children missing, I knew what had happened. The rapture had come and I had been left behind."

"Wait!" Said Josie, "you describe yourself as being a good Christian. If you were a good Christian, why were you left behind?"

"OK I will tell you why I got left behind," said Deacon Bill. "The people in this church always had respect for me, they called me Deacon Bill, and they thought I was really a holy person. They would call me to pray with them, and counsel with them on spiritual matters. My wife and I had a perfect marriage; we had brought our children up in the nurture and admonition of the Lord. We had a perfect family. Then something happened. A lady called me over to her house for counseling, she said she had a real problem, and needed some spiritual help. I had been trained if I was going to counsel with a woman to always take someone with me. This day there wasn't anyone around to go with me. I could have waited until my wife or some other man was available, but I thought I was strong in the Lord, so I could handle things. When I went into her house she was dressed real sexy, that is when I should have run, but I didn't. I sat down and begin to counsel her. She told me she and her husband were having marriage problems, she said he wasn't giving her the love she needed, and then she begins to cry. I went over to comfort her, I put my arms around her to comfort her, and she pulled me close to her. One thing led to another, and we committed adultery.

I begin to feel ashamed of myself, I asked God to forgive me for what I had done, and I know he did. But Satan would try to tell me God didn't love me any more and he hadn't forgiven me. I would tell Satan he was a liar for God had said in his holy word "if we confess our sins, he will forgive our sins and cleanse us from all unrighteousness." I knew without a doubt Jesus had forgiven me. The devil didn't leave me alone though after that. He would entice me time after time to commit sin. The Holy Spirit would try to speak to me. At first I would listen to him. But then when the devil would keep enticing me I would finally give in to him. I knew I was grieving the Holy Spirit.

The Holy Spirit finally left me to do what I willed. I knew what I was doing was wrong, and I knew I was living a lie

Revival Of Those Left Behind

before my wife and family. I knew if I didn't quit what I was doing, my wife would find out and our marriage would be over. I wouldn't only ruin my life, but would ruin my wife's life, and hurt my children, and grandchildren. My wife was a good wife, my children had followed in my footsteps, and my grandchildren loved their grandpa. I would say every time, I am going to break off this relationship, but would fall into the devils trap again. I do not want to make it sound as if Jesus doesn't have power to help us overcome these things, he was always casting the devil out of people when he was on the earth, and demons are cast out today in his name through the Holy Spirit, but he did want me to put up some resistance. He said in his word, "Draw near to God, resist the devil and he will flee from you." Now look what has happened to me, the rapture has come, my wife children and grandchildren are gone to be with Jesus.

Here I am left behind. The woman I was seeing is still around, but I have made up my mind, by the help of Jesus I will never go around her again. I know I will have to say no to the antichrist and refuse his mark and will be persecuted for it, but what ever it takes from now on I will be faithful to my Lord. I do know God can forgive this lady as same as he can me, I just hope she will turn to God.

Please forgive me for taking up so much of your time. I would be glad to have a Bible study with you folks. When will we start? Do we want to study in our homes or here at the church?"

"I think it would be good to study here at the church," said Josie. "There might be others here with us today that would like to study with us." "Good idea," said Deacon Bill. "I will ask them." He goes to the podium, and asks for the people's attention. Everyone gets very quite, because they think he has some news for them about the rapture. He said, "There are some folks here who have mentioned having a Bible study to learn what the Bible said about the end times, would any of you like to join our study?" Everyone said in unison yes! Deacon Bill we would like to join the study group. Some of the people that were there that day knew Deacon Bill, but they didn't question why he was left behind, because they like him had missed the mark. Deacon Bill noticed that most of them didn't have their Bible with them, he suggested everyone go home, have breakfast or lunch come back at 1:00 p.m. and be sure to bring their Bibles.

Stan and Josie say bye to everyone and head for home. On the way home they are really excited about the Bible study Josie said to Stan, "I sure am glad we went over to the Agape Church. I believe we are going to get some answers now about where our children are."

Stan said, "Yes, I think going over to Agape Church is the best thing we have done today. I think this Deacon Bill knows the Bible and will give us some answers."

Chapter 4

REPORT FROM WASHINGTON

Stan and Josie arrive home; Stan turns on the TV, while Josie prepares lunch. The local reporter is reporting bad news all over. He said, "Some of the main highway bridges are shut down because of accidents. One bridge that carries thousands of cars and trucks in a day is in a mess. A truck carrying flammable has gone out of control; it has caught fire and is burning. The heat is threatening the structure of the bridge. Many cars and other trucks are either wrecked or stuck on the bridge. There is a report of two trains running together, one is a freight train, and the other is a passenger train. The freight train was supposed to take a side track to let the passenger train pass by. For some reason the freight train failed to take the siding. The passenger train had tried to reach the engineer by cell phone, but was unable to reach him, so thinking he was on the siding the passenger train engineer kept going at a high speed. Now most of the cars are derailed in a mass of twisted steel. Emergency crews [that were few] are trying to rescue the passengers. They are plagued with another problem. The freight train was carrying several cars, with hazardous material. It is leaking out of some of the cars. The captain of the rescue crew has described it as a real mess. There is also a report of a train, which was descending down a mountain grade for some reason unknown at this time the train begins to pick up speed, and had reached speeds of up to 200 miles an hour, before it reached a sharp curve, where it derailed and devastated a mountain community. Someone has said that they had seen the train going by at a high speed, and it didn't look like there was anyone in the cab. We would like to take you to Washington DC at this time where our Washington correspondent is standing by.

Go ahead Hal what have you got for us. "Thanks Ann we will bring you up to date on what is happening here. Things are a real mess! I believe at this time we have one of the President's aides present who is going to tell us what is happening, and where the President is."

"Good morning fellow citizens. I will try to bring you up to date what is going on here in Washington. No one has seen the President. They have searched everywhere in the white house, and he cannot be found anywhere. His limo is in the garage, his helicopter is on its pad, and the airport has reported his plane on the ground. Some of the secret service who guards the President is missing. Those that are here are worried about what is going to happen to them if someone has taken the President during the night. His wife is also missing. Whoever took him must have taken his wife also.

The President was a very religious man. The President had mentioned at different times that he thought we were living in the last days. Sometimes when there was a crisis, he would say; it would be nice if Jesus would come today. He had said Jesus could solve the world problems that he could not solve. He had mentioned a time when Jesus would take the true believers out of this world. I do not believe this is our answer to where the President is, I don't know how he could have left the white house. It couldn't be terrorists or aliens from another planet; our security is too secure for that to happen. One of the Senators has made mention that the President may have slipped out in secret during the night, the Senator said the President keeps a lot of secrets, and he can't be trusted. That couldn't be true as security is too tight for that. Some others are saying this rapture idea that some people are mentioning is just a lot of baloney.

They say these prophecy preachers who have been preaching Jesus is coming as a thief in the night and take out the believers is just something they have dreamed up, they say, these prophecy preachers made a big thing out of Y2K. What happened then? Absolutely nothing happened. We have been trying to reach some of these well known prophecy preachers, to see what they have to say about what is going on, but we have been unable to get in touch with them. No one answers the phone at his or her headquarters.

This one thing we do know. There are people missing all over the world. It looks like the most people are missing from Christian nations. It has been reported that many of our air controllers are missing, and many pilots are missing from their planes, leaving their planes to crash. Here is a radio message that was received from one of the flight attendants on a plane listen as we play it for you.

'This is Helen on flight no 777, I do not know what is going on up here, but I am really scared. Some of our passengers have vanished, they are not in the rest rooms, and there is no where else they could be. I have tried to talk to the pilot, or co-pilot on the intercom, they will not answer me, oh God! What is going on? Oh God! Our plane is going down, oh God! What am I going to do all the people on this plane have panicked? They are saying they don't want to die. One lady want's to know what has happened to her baby, oh God! How am I supposed to know? People are crying all over the plane. We are going to try to get into the cockpit to see what is going on in there now. Oh my, oh my! The pilot and co-pilot aren't up here, where are they, oh God what are we going to do? Tower, tower can you help us none of us know how to fly this plane, we have had some training in flying, but who could remember what to do in a time like this, oh God I am scared!"

"Helen this is the tower, we are short handed today, but I will try my best to get you down, what is your location, I don't have you on my radar screen."

"Location, oh me, how am I supposed to know?"

"Just read your gages and they will tell you."

"Tower this is Helen I am loosing altitude real fast, I think we are going to crash! Oh God what can I do!"

"Helen this is the tower, don't panic, and just listen to me. Pull back on your control stick to level the plane off."

"Ok," said Helen, "we are leveling off, now what?"

"Ok Helen now put the plane on auto pilot; this will hold the altitude you are flying. We will try to figure out where you are; maybe we can get you down somewhere. By the way how much fuel do you have left?"

"Oh no, Not much!" said Helen, "what are we going to do?'

"Just hang on said the controller, I have to get another plane landed and I will be right back with you."

"Be sure you don't forget about us," said Helen.

A few minutes later Helen is crying out, "tower! Tower! Our engines are sputtering, oh God they are quitting! We are going down!" Helen is heard crying out to God. "God I do believe you are real. I do believe you died for my sins,

God please save me. I repent of all my sins." The screams throughout the plane is getting louder and louder, most of the people are calling on God. The last thing that was heard on flight 777 was a great explosion. "I am very sorry this ended this way," said the President's aide.

It is reported said the aide that our military is in chaos, but I am going to let a representative of our armed forces address this matter. Here is General Lee Hall"

"Good morning fellow citizens this is General Lee Hall. I do not know all the details on everything that is going on, but I do know our military is in a total mess at this present time. We have reports of planes crashing on take off, some crashing while landing, planes and helicopters falling from mid air. The mystery to this whole thing is no one has been able to find the pilots of the planes after they have crashed, and none of the planes have reported any problems in flight. We have reports of military personnel missing throughout the world. We have a report from the battle fields; they say the enemy is about to overrun our forces because thousand's of our troops have deserted.

One of the soldiers has reported what he saw; he said some of the troops in his group just vanished dropping their guns to the ground, only he and a very few had been left to fight the battle, he reports watching some of the tanks passing right by the enemy without shooting their guns. Some had just been blown up with out even putting up a fight, some of our support planes have been shot down, or have just crash landed. Some of them passed over the enemy and didn't even fire their guns. They crashed after they had passed over the enemy. He said, it is bad out here, we are so outnumbered, I don't think we can hold out much longer; please send us some help! We lost contact with him after that.

One of our planes transporting troops has completely disappeared. We had tried to reach the pilot by radio, when he had disappeared on our radar screen, but were unable to reach him. We will continue to try to reach him. I know our information isn't good news, we don't really know just what is going on. I do know this a lot of our military that were on the battle field were very religious, and if there was such a thing as Jesus coming for the church he would have taken them out. What I do not know is why he would take them out, and let the enemy overrun our troops. I am going to turn this back to the spokesman for the President at this time. When we have more information we will let you know."

"This is your Washington correspondent. You have heard from the President's aide, and General Hall. They haven't given us any good news. We are going to return you to your local programming."

"Ok thanks Tom this is Ann from YLTS reporting. We have been trying to get one of our local pastors on the line. I am sure they will know what is going on. We now have Pastor Joe, pastor of the Ladoci church on the line. Hi Pastor Joe, welcome to our program. You are one of our outstanding and knowledgeable pastors in our city. We hope you can explain to our listeners just what has been going on."

"Thanks for having me on your program," said Pastor Joe, "I will be happy to answer any questions I can."

"Pastor Joe we woke up this morning to the shock of our lives, many of our loved ones were missing, no one so far has been able to explain to us just what has occurred. We are sure you have the answers."

"Well I am not real sure what has taken place, but I do know it doesn't have anything to do with Jesus taking the Christians to heaven. I know the Bible does speak about the Christians going to heaven in the last days, but we are not living in the last days. You just look at the times we are living in. Our people are living prosperous lives; they have nice homes, automobiles, boats, ATV's, and all kinds of pleasure. Our church is doing well. We have just had a big expansion program. We had it paid for as soon as it was built, we have a lot of wealthy people in our church, and our church doesn't have need of anything. God is sure blessing our church. I don't think for one minute he would leave us behind. I cannot explain just where all the people have gone, but I do think when we find out it will probable have to do with aliens from another planet. We are seeing things like this happening in some of our movies everyday."

"Pastor Joe let me break in for a moment. We have been trying to reach some of the pastors that are more conservative. We have talked to someone in his or her church; they tell us the pastor is missing like a lot of the people from their church. How do you explain this? Why would someone from another planet take them and not take you?"

"I think God may have taken them out of this life, because they have been preaching a false doctrine."

"Ok Pastor Joe why do you think they have been preaching a false doctrine? What have they been preaching different from what you preach?"

"They preach grace with works. I preach grace without works."

"Pastor Joe, could you explain to us what you mean by this?"

"Sure said Pastor Joe, they teach after you accept Christ, you have to live a Holy life. I teach grace saves us and it doesn't make any difference what kind of life you live."

"Ok Pastor Joe, thank you for being on our program. We do hope we can speak to you again as soon as more news develops."

"Sure," said Pastor Joe, "anytime and thanks for having me on the program."

Stan said, "Josie have you noticed what time it is? No said Josie,

"I guess the time has gotten away from us, it is almost one o'clock. We had better hurry to the Bible study." "Yes," said Stan, "by all means, we sure don't want to be late." They hurry out to their car and leave for the Agape Church.

Chapter 5

BIBLE STUDY AGAPE CHURCH

S tan and Josie arrive at Agape Church. Deacon Bill greets them and asks if they were ready to begin the study. "Sure," they say, "we are sorry if we are a little late, but we were listening to our pastor on the news. He doesn't seem to know anything. We are anxious to get started. As soon as you are ready we are ready." Mary and her husband Paul and several others had already arrived at the church.

Deacon Bill goes to the podium, and begins to address the people. He said, "I am Deacon Bill one of the deacons of this church. Which I am ashamed to say because I have let my Lord down, and I have been left behind. I will explain this more as we go along in our study. I awoke this morning to sirens, and dogs barking. I noticed my wife had already gotten up, [or I thought she had]. When I began to look for her in the house she wasn't anywhere to be found. I thought for sure she had found out about me being unfaithful, and had left me. I looked in the garage to see if her car was gone, but to my surprise it was in the garage. I ran back in the house and phoned our daughter to see if she knew where her mother was, I could only get her answering machine. I tried to phone our son, but only got his answering machine. I thought something strange is sure going on. I thought maybe my wife was still in the bedroom, or had been in the closet.

When I began to look, I noticed her night clothes were still under the blanket. I thought for a minute, why did she leave her night clothes under the blanket, and then I noticed something else was strange. Her clothes she had laid out before going to bed were still lying where she had put them. I really began to worry, and think where is everybody? I went in and turned on the TV. The news person was saying people were missing all over the world. As soon as I heard that I knew for sure what had taken place. The rapture had come and I had been left behind.

Pastor John our pastor had preached many times about the soon coming of the Lord. He had said all the Bible prophecies were fulfilled right up to the rapture of the church. He had said the Bible said Jesus will come as a thief in the night, and he would be coming at a time we think not. He always told us to be ready.

I suppose some of you are wondering, why has Deacon Bill been left behind if Jesus has come in the rapture? I suppose I should address that question at this time. Jesus taught us that he was coming for a church without spot or wrinkle [sinless church]. I had been living a lie. I had committed a sinful act. I do know the Bible said Jesus died on the cross for our sins. I believe he had forgiven me of my sins. The Bible said in John; 'if we confess our sins, he [Jesus] is faithful and just to forgive us our sins, and cleanse us from all unrighteousness."

The problem was I kept telling Jesus I was going to start living a better life, but I kept on doing the same things over and over again. I had grieved the Holy Spirit and he had

Revival Of Those Left Behind

left me. I don't think I am doomed for hell, but I do know I have missed the rapture, and now am going to have to go through the great tribulation period. It isn't going to be easy, but I am determined I will hold out faithful to the Lord unto death. This is enough about me; now let us get on with our study. Has anyone got any questions before we begin?"

"Yes," said Josie, "you have been mentioning the word rapture a lot. Pastor Joe over at the Ladoci church where we have been attending said the Bible doesn't even mention rapture. How do you explain this? Does the Bible say anything about a rapture of the church?"

"I will try to answer your question," said Deacon Bill. "Pastor Joe is correct the Bible doesn't mention the word rapture, but it mentions being caught up to meet the Lord in the air. The word rapture means caught out or up. This is what we mean when we mention rapture. The apostle Paul mentions in [I Thessalonians 4:13-18.] about Jesus descending from heaven. The dead rising first, and we that are alive and remain being caught up with them in the clouds, and forever being with the Lord. We will go into this in more detail a little later. But first let's talk about the second coming of Christ.

In the Old Testament the prophets had prophesied that God would raise up a king like King David. They had prophesied where he would be born, how he would be born, [virgin] and many other things. When Jesus came to this earth he was the one that would fulfill the prophecies, and he does in the book of revelation. But in the days Christ was upon the earth the religious leaders didn't understand the scriptures.

They didn't understand that before he would be king of kings and Lord of Lords he would have to go to the cross, die for our sins, rise again on the third day, and then ascend back to heaven, sit on the right hand of the Father, and remain there until the Father would send him to get the church that was looking for his coming. He would catch the righteous out to heaven, then the antichrist would come on the scene, the world would go into a time of tribulation like it had never witnessed before.

The Bible said in revelation [Chapter 13:7-8.] "And it was given to him [antichrist] to make war with the saints and to overcome them; and power was given him over all kindred, tongues, and nations, and all that dwell upon the earth shall worship him [antichrist]. Whose names are not written in the book of life of the lamb slain from the foundation of the world" In the first three and one half years of the rule of the antichrist, many Christians, which had been following Jesus at a distant, would begin to serve him with all of their heart; they would refuse the mark of the beast, and be killed. This is something many preachers today do not fully understand. They say I don't study prophecy. It is too deep for me. So since the preachers don't study prophecy, or allow it to be taught in their church, and since it is not taught, many people in the church fail to understand it.

If we study very carefully we will notice that there is two phases to the coming of the Lord. One is "rapture," when he comes in the clouds for the church, and takes them to heaven, where they will participates in the marriage of the lamb. This is when Jesus gets married to the church. The marriage is found in revelation the 19 Chapter. The other coming is when he comes to the earth as King of Kings and Lord of Lords to rule a thousand years. Also found in revelations Chapter 19.

Now let us talk a little more about the rapture. Turn to [I Thessalonians 4:13-18] "but I would not have you to be ignorant, brethren, concerning them which are asleep, that you sorrow not, even as others which have no hope". Let's stop there, and take this portion of scripture one verse at a time. Notice in verse thirteen he is telling them to not sorrow over those who are asleep, [those who have laid off their earthly body which has been buried, and their spirit and soul has gone to be with Jesus.] Jesus said in the gospel of John "I am the resurrection and the life, he that believeth in me, though he be dead, [asleep] yet shall he live; and whosoever liveth and believeth in me shall never die."

In the book of Ecclesiastes, the word said this, "the dust goes back to the earth, and the spirit goes back to God who gave it". In study of the Bible it appears if a Christian dies his soul goes with the spirit to heaven, but if the person isn't a Christian his soul goes to hell. Now let's look at [verse 14,] "for if we believe Jesus died and rose again, even so God will bring with Him those who sleep in Jesus". This is saying if we believe Jesus died on the cross, was buried again and then rose from the dead, [to be a Christian we must believe this.] When Jesus comes again for the church he will be bringing the spirit and soul back with him to be reunited with the elements of the body, which is sleeping in the grave. [Verse 15]; "for this we say unto you by the word of the Lord, that we which are alive and remain unto the coming of the Lord shall not prevent them which are asleep". This is simply telling us the ones who have already died will go first.

Now [verse 16], "for the Lord himself shall descend from heaven with a shout, with the voice of the archangel, and with the trump of God; and the dead in Christ will rise first." Be sure to notice here who is going to rise first. "The dead in Christ" take careful note of the in Christ. The book of revelation speaks about the first resurrection. The first resurrection is for those who are in Christ. There is a second resurrection which takes place just before the great white throne judgment. [This is for the wicked dead] now go to [verse 16] "then we which are alive and remain shall be caught up together with them in the clouds, to meet the Lord in the air; and so shall we ever be with the Lord." This is talking about those whom are in Christ, and are still living.

Lets notice another thing in this verse, both the dead in Christ and the alive in Christ are going to meet the Lord in the air, this said he isn't going to set foot on earth at this coming, but when he comes as Lord of Lords and king of kings he will set his foot on the mount of olives. Now look at [verse 18]; "wherefore comfort one another with these words." At that time many of the Christians were being killed because of their faith in Christ. Paul wrote this letter telling them to take comfort because their loved ones would rise again in the resurrection.

We would like to point out to you based on scripture in other parts of the Bible. When Jesus comes in the rapture, he will come for Christians who are being faithful to him. He will say to them, "You have been faithful in a few things, enter in the joy of the Lord". Jesus spoke about Christians being left behind in the parable of the ten virgins, Recorded in the gospel of Matthew Chapter 25. Is there any questions?"

"Yes I have a question," said Josie. "If the scripture said the dead in Christ shall rise first, and you say we that remain, which are in Christ shall be caught up together with them in the clouds to meet the Lord in the air. Would you explain a little more in detail what the Bible means when it is talking about the dead in Christ. Who are the dead in Christ, and who is the wicked dead?"

"Yes", said Deacon Bill. "I will be glad to explain this. First let's deal with those who are in Christ. The ones who are in Christ are those who have received Jesus into their life and have been "born again." Jesus spoke about new birth in the gospel of John in his conversation with Nichodemus. Paul spoke about being in Christ in [II Corinthians 5:17] lets read this scripture. "Therefore if any man be in Christ, he is a new creature [creation]: old things are passed away; behold all things are become new."

Peter said in [I peter 1:23]. "Being born again, not of corruptible seed, but of incorruptible, by the Word of God." John said in [I John 5:1] "whosoever believeth that Jesus is the Christ is born of God." John wrote in his gospel [John 1:12-13] "but as many as received him, to them gave he power to become the sons of God, even to them that believe on his name: which were born, not of blood, nor of the will of the flesh, but of God." Now let's try to explain what we have been quoting. When we believe the word of God his seed is planted in us. Then the seed needs to be watered by hearing more of the word. When we begin to exercise our faith, and believe Gods word we begin to believe Jesus is Gods son; we begin to believe in his life, death, resurrection and ascension. We begin to understand why he went to the cross, and why he died for our sins. We begin to realize we are a sinner, and we cannot save our self, and the only way we can be saved is through Jesus' death on the cross. We receive Jesus as our Lord and savior; God begins to cause the seed that has been planted in us to sprout and to grow.

At this time we become a new creation in Christ. The Holy Spirit comes into our life and begins to lead and to guide us in all ways of truth and right. He directs us to study the word, and pray. He leads us in getting rid of the old sinful man, and to put on the new man. When we begin to quench the spirit [that is not to listen to him] he is grieved because he is trying to help us live a good life. Maybe we can get into this some more at a later time.

Now quickly let's explain those who are not in Christ. These are the ones who have heard the gospel, but have procrastinated in inviting Jesus into their life and have hardened their hearts by letting Satan and sin deceive them. Jesus said, "They will not come to the light, because they love darkness rather than light." Jesus' talked about coming to his own and his own receiving him not. He was talking about the Jews at that time, but when he talked about as many as receive Him He was also talking to the gentiles [none Jews] [John 3:16] said: "for God so loved the world, that he gave his only begotten son, that whosoever believeth in him should not perish, but have everlasting life." Jesus died for everybody, but only those which will believe and come to him will be saved.

I suppose we should take a break at this time, I think we are all getting a little tired. I would like to suggest we take a break until 7:00 P.M., and then we will take up the study of the ten virgins."

Everyone agrees this will be fine, Deacon Bill has a prayer, they have some fellowship, and discuss some of the things they have heard, then Deacon Bill said, "If you have loved ones, friends, or neighbors who have been left behind, invite them to the study tonight."

Stan and Josie, leave for home. They talk about the things they have heard in the Bible study. Josie said, "Stan I am not sure at this time if I have ever received Christ into my life. I know we went forward and joined the church over at Ladoci and begin attending church most of the time. But I am thinking I never truly got saved."

Stan said, "You know I have been thinking the same thing."

Josie said, "I think I am going to invite Jesus into my heart tonight."

"Yes" said Stan, I think I will do the same."

Chapter 6

STAN AND JOSIE RETURN HOME

S tan and Josie go into the house. They call out for the children, but get no answer. Josie said to Stan, "it is so lonesome around here without the children." She begins to cry and said; "I don't know if I can take it any longer. I loved our children so much, we were always thrilled when they would come running to us, putting their arms around us and saying I love you."

Stan puts his arms around Josie, and said, "I miss the children very much also; they were my pride and joy. I wish they were here but since we have been in this Bible study, I feel better about them not being here. I feel the rapture has really taken place. Jesus has come and taken our children with him to be with him in heaven. They are probably sitting at the feet of Jesus, and he is teaching them. They are probably surrounded by thousands of other children. They are probably happier than they have ever been. They had studied about Jesus loving the little children now they are there with him for him to show his love for them. They will never fall and hurt themselves again. They will never be sick again, neither will they see death. They have entered into the joy of the Lord. I wouldn't want to bring them back to this sinful world. I just wish we could be with them.

Since we can't be with them, I think it is good to know we can go where they are. According to Deacon Bill if we turn our life over to Christ, start serving him, refuse to worship the antichrist, refuse the mark, we will be able to go be with them in a matter of weeks or months."

"Yes," said Josie, "I do believe this, but I don't know why we didn't study our Bible and learn about this before it was too late. Why didn't I listen more to what Maria had to say. Why was I so stubborn, Maria has prayed for you and me many times. She tried to get us to get in a Bible believing Church; of course we always thought our church was just as good as the church she went to. We thought our pastor was preaching the truth. We had our Bibles, we even took our Bibles to church, but we never took the time to read what God was saying to us. Maria used to tell me what their pastor had preached on the prior Sunday. Sometimes it was getting saved, sometimes it was about living a holy life, sometimes it would be about Jesus coming again, and the ones that would be left behind, and sometimes it would be the antichrist. Sometimes I would get mad at her, and call her a holy roller I would tell her to butt off, and mind her own business.

She would just say, Josie I love you. You are my friend. If you weren't my friend I wouldn't come to see you all the time. Sometimes I would get very angry with her, and tell her I didn't want to ever see her again. She would say, Please don't be that way Josie, we have been friends all our lives. We went to school together, we grew up together, and we graduated at the same time from high school. You was the maid of honor at my wedding, we have seen our families grow up together. I am sorry if I have offended you, I only tell you about these things because I love you, and want you to be in heaven with me. I would think within my self, why doesn't she mind her own business. One day I was so angry at her that I begin to scream at her and ask her to leave; I called her every bad word I could think of. She said I am very sorry Josie; please forgive me if I have offended you. She left my house crying. I would think how dare you for apologizing, why didn't you just scream back at me, and then I would feel justified for my actions.

We would make up although; I don't remember me ever apologizing to her. She was the one to apologize. Why was I so stubborn? Why didn't I listen to her? If I would have listened to her, I would be with her today and with my children. This is the hardest thing I have ever had to bare. I am like Deacon Bill. I want to go be with Jesus, and with my children, but I am afraid I haven't invited Jesus into my heart."

Stan and Josie sat down on the couch. They are cuddling, and comforting each other. They turn on the TV, to find everything is still about those missing. The news commentator said it has been pretty well determined that terrorist, or aliens from outer space have had nothing to do with people being missing, but the Secret Service, and Home Land Security are still investigating. As soon as they have something concrete they will let the people know. Some of the preachers are still saying it is not the rapture of the church. Of course a lot of the preachers are not available to talk about it. Some of the churches are having Bible studies trying to determine if it is the rapture.

Some are teaching it is for sure the rapture of the church. They are saying if it is not true Jesus has caught out the church. Why is all the smaller children, and the teens and adults which were living a righteous life missing? And why are the people who weren't living a righteous life still here? We do know this for certain the world is in complete chaos. It seems like the USA has more problems, than anyone else. It is not known how many people are dead and wounded in the United States, but there already has been reported thousands dead. In most all of our hospitals they are reporting a shortage of staff. The emergency rooms are overfilled with patients, some patients are lying in the floor, and blood is everywhere. There is a shortage of paramedics to bring the people in to the hospitals. They have to let the dead lie, so as to take care of the wounded. People are bringing the wounded in to the emergency in their cars. Some of the morgues are reporting they cannot take in any more bodies. It is reported that most of our interstates in the larger cities are at a   standstill because of accidents. They have been this way since this morning; it is not known when they will be able to open again. There doesn't seem to be enough tow trucks to clean up the mess. The airports are all shut down, except for incoming planes. The federal government said they will be shut down until further notice. None of the subways in the large cities are running, they are still trying to clear up the wreckage, and rescue the wounded, and retrieve the dead. Many of the railroads are still shut down trying to clean up all the wreckage. There has been a recent report of a large explosion, caused from a leaking chemical spill from a rail car. The train had derailed and was leaking chemicals from more than one tanker; one was burning furiously. The few firemen that could be mustered were trying to put out the flames, chemicals from one of the other cars leaked over to be ignited by the flames causing a large explosion, which has devastated several blocks. The flames from the home fires are leaping to other homes.

There aren't enough firemen or water pressure to fight the flames. The firemen who were fighting the fire at the chemical spill were killed in the explosion; also people were killed several blocks from the explosion. We will report on what is happening at this scene, as soon as we know more about it. It looks like the ships have fared better than the other means of transportation, although there has been reports of some accidents in our ports which has been minor considering the other means of transportation, I think we are going to take a break for a little while said the news commentator, I have been here all day without any relief. We have had a skeleton crew all day. Some of our personnel who are still around will not come in because of their family members being missing. I can say this; this is the worse day the world has known in my lifetime. Ok we will be back later."

Josie said to Stan, "do you want me to fix some dinner?"

"No," said Stan, "I just don't seem to be hungry, we can snack if we get hungry lets just try to relax for a little before going back to the Bible study."

"Sounds good to me," said Josie; "I am not hungry for food, but I can't wait to go back to the Bible study.

"Josie I was just thinking about some of our neighbors," said Stan; "when we were out this morning they were saying they had loved ones missing also. We wouldn't be very good neighbors if we didn't share with them some of the things, we have learned in Bible study today."

"Sure," said Josie; "let's share with them and invite them to the Bible study tonight."

Stan and Josie go to their neighbors and begin to share with them about the Bible study they have been attending that afternoon at the Agape Church; and they also tell them about the study at 7:00 p.m. Some are very receptive and thank them for inviting them to the Bible study, and say they will think about the Bible study, but are not sure they want to attend.

Then there were those that said, "We don't believe in your religion. We don't want any part of a God that would come and take our children from us; we don't believe this baloney about a rapture taken place."

Although they didn't believe in the rapture of the church, none of them could give a good reason why their loved ones were missing. They still have hope the children will reappear. Stan and Josie would apologize to them and tell them they are sorry they had mentioned it. Stan and Josie go home and relax for a little before going to the evening Bible study.

Chapter 7

TEN VIRGINS

Stan and Josie arrive at the church for the seven o'clock Bible study. Deacon Bill was waiting for everyone to arrive. The church was almost full, and people were still coming. Deacon Bill had asked the ushers to put out as many folding chairs as possible. Those chairs were just about filled and people were still coming. Deacon Bill cautioned the ushers to not let the people block the aisles or the exits, and it would be wise to close the doors, and not let anyone else in. Deacon Bill promised them the Bible study would be held again the next morning at 9:30 for those who couldn't get in. He said tomorrow morning he was going to teach the same thing he was teaching tonight. Stan and Josie had already seen some of their neighbors in the crowd. Other people had also invited their friends, and relatives.

Deacon Bill begins to speak, "he welcomes everyone to the study. He said, I will do my best to explain the scriptures to you, but I wish our pastor was here because he could do a better job than me. But I wouldn't want to call him back from heaven. He was a wonderful pastor, and always preached the word. He was a hard worker, and he deserves everything Jesus has prepared for him in heaven.

I feel a little like he was Lazarus, [the poor beggar that the angels carried to paradise] and I am the rich man who died and went to hell. Although I was not rich and thank God I haven't died. Ok that is enough about me, now let's talk about Jesus and the parable he gave us in his word about the ten virgins

We have mentioned there are two phases of the coming of Christ. One is when he comes in the rapture, and the other is when he comes as King of Kings and Lord of Lords. I guess if we study the book of Revelation, there is also those Christians who are left behind who are caught up during the tribulation period, and the 144,000 Jews who are sealed during the tribulation period. Let us now go to [Matthew 25:1-13,] and study about the ten virgins. If we were to go back to the 24th Chapter we would find Jesus was discussing signs of his coming. It would be a good idea for you to read the 24th Chapter when you get home tonight.

Now let's look at verse 1 of the 25th Chapter. Jesus said; "then shall the kingdom of heaven be likened to ten virgins, which took their lamps, and went forth to meet the bridegroom." Jesus is comparing the kingdom of heaven to a wedding. He is comparing his coming to a bridegroom who is coming for his bride. Of course we know the bride of Christ is the church. We will find the wedding supper taking place in revelation Chapter 19, verses 7 thru 9. You can read that scripture later. Notice they were virgins. This would represent purity. Virgins are young ladies that have kept themselves pure for their wedding day. We are taught in the Bible that we are made pure through the precious blood of Jesus, which was shed on Calvary's cross. We are the church. Now another thing we notice about these ten virgins, they have lights, or lamps. Jesus said he was the light of the world, and those who follow him shall not walk in darkness. When we become Christians we become pure,

Revival Of Those Left Behind

and he puts his light in us. We begin to reflect his light to this dark world.

Now we notice in the 2nd verse Jesus said: "and five were wise and five were foolish". I believe he was saying when he comes in the rapture there will be some Christians who are wise and some who are foolish.

Now let's go to the verse 3. Jesus said; "they that were foolish took no oil with them," and verse 4 said; "but the wise took oil in their vessels with their lamps." Oil in this parable would represent the substance that was needed to keep their lamps burning. When we compare this with spiritual things it would be the oil of the Spirit, which is needed to keep our lights shining in this dark world. If we do not have the spirit leading us in this old sinful world, we will not be able to stand.

Verse 5 reads; "while the bridegroom tarried they all slumbered and slept." We notice they all slumbered and slept, but there was a big difference in the five foolish and the five wise. The wise had oil to keep their lamps burning, so they could relax, but not so with the foolish. They should have been aware that if the bride [Jesus] were to come that night they would not be ready. Their sins had probably caused the Holy Spirit to be grieved and he had probably left them alone because they were continuing to live in their sins, without asking Jesus to forgive them. Some of us here tonight are in the category with the foolish virgins, he has come and we have been left behind,

Notice verse 6; "and at midnight there was a cry made, behold the bridegroom cometh, go ye out to meet him". He has come in the night and it was a night that the foolish virgins didn't think he would come, but the cry came unexpected, go ye out to meet him, then it was too late to think about getting the oil. The Bible said he will come in a moment, in the twinkling of the eye. That is pretty fast

Go to the 7th verse, "then all those virgins arose and trimmed their lamps". Some of you that are younger, may not know what he is talking about, I will try to explain: Back in the days before electricity everyone used lamps to give them light. The lamps had cloth wicks, which went down into the oil; the oil would go up the wick to where the flame would be lit to give the light. If you were to let the oil run low, the wick would burn on one side causing it to smoke up the globe on the lamp. This caused the light to not give its light properly. When the oil had been replenished the wick would have to be trimmed. In the case of the foolish virgins it didn't do any good to trim the wick, there was no oil to keep the lamp going.

Notice what the foolish said to the wise in verse 8, "and the foolish said unto the wise, give us of your oil for our lamps have gone out." I remember an old song which goes like this, "oh how lonely, oh how sad if the light has gone out in your soul" when I was a boy it was one of the most important things, when we went into town to make sure we had a good supply of oil, if our lamp would run out of oil, we couldn't even see to get around the house. We were like a blind man trying to feel our way around the house and to the bed. Probably some of you may have experienced something similar, when the electricity would go off at night, and you had no flashlight, or candles.

Let's look at the answer the foolish give them in verse 9, "But the wise answered, saying, not so, lest there be not enough for us and you, but go ye rather to them that sell, and buy for yourselves." We cannot give other people our salvation; our mothers, fathers, children, or anybody can't give us their salvation. It is free, it is a gift, but we must go to the one who has purchased it for us. His name is Jesus! We cannot give anyone ours, but we can point them to the one that has it. [Jesus]

Now notice the 10th verse, "and while they went to buy, the bridegroom came. They that were ready went in with him to the marriage; and the door was shut." This verse said to me, you can't wait until you hear the sound of Jesus' coming to make things right. This teaches we are to be ready at all times, and serving him. It is not enough to just know Jesus we must serve him. Notice those that were ready went in with him to the marriage and the door was shut. No one else could go in but those that were ready. I do not believe this is saying no one else will get to go to heaven, but no one else will get to go in at the rapture. Let us look at the next verse it indicates they did get oil after he had come, but were too late for the rapture.

[Verse 11]: "afterward came; also the other virgins, saying, Lord, Lord. Open to us." It indicates here, they did find oil [the Holy Spirit] they were now ready, but the rapture had taken place. We do believe they will have to go into the tribulation period, and be killed by the antichrist.

[Revelation 13:7] said, "And it was given to him [the antichrist] to make war with the saints and to overcome them." I believe this is talking about the five foolish virgins [Christians that are not taking up their cross, and following Jesus], and some people, which have heard the gospel. And have all intentions of accepting Christ, but have been putting it off, have decided now that they will serve God regardless of the cost to them. Then there are those who have hardened their hearts toward the gospel, and don't even want to hear about the gospel, they will become more hardened when the rapture takes place. They will shake their fist in Gods face, and blame him for taking their children, and loved ones. They will join the antichrist in searching out and killing the Christians.

Now let's go back to the virgins in [verse 12]. "But he answered and said verily [or truly} I know you not. He is not saying I never knew you, but I know you not. I think he is saying your sins have caused you to be hidden from me at this time. Their lamps were not burning when he came, so he couldn't see them. If you followed me closely you will have discovered I have put the ones left behind in three different categories. No 1, the foolish virgins. No 2 those who are studying the word, but haven't made a decision, and No.3, those who have hardened their hearts against the church and the gospel. Now let's go into the three categories a little more in detail:

Category number one look at [Luke 12:45-46] "but and if that servant said in his heart, my Lord delayeth his coming and shall begin to beat his manservant, and his maidservant, and eat and drink, to be drunken; the Lord of that servant will come in a day when he looketh not for him, and an hour when he is not aware, and will cut him asunder, and will appoint him his portion with the unbelievers." This would be the foolish virgins.

Now let's go to category two: Apostle Paul when referring to the rapture mentioned the ones who were in Christ, those in category two have never accepted Christ, so they are not in Christ. Jesus is only coming for those in Christ at the rapture.

Now let's move to category three: In [Psalms 95] God mentioned those who had hardened their heart when Moses was leading them through the wilderness, they were not able to go into the promise land. He tells this generation to not harden our heart. If we do we will not be able to enter into his rest. This is the ones in category three who have been hardened by the gospel and don't want to hear about Jesus.

It is getting late so we want to wind up our study for tonight soon, but before we go let us finish the study on the virgins.

[verse13] "Watch therefore, for ye know neither the day nor the hour wherein the son of man cometh." [Referring to Jesus coming] We do know he has come and found us not watching.

We who are here tonight have fallen into category one and category two. We have all been foolish for not watching. If the foolish virgins had only been watching, and looking for the Lord they would have been living for the Lord instead of for themselves. I can say to you this is the category I was in this morning, but I have already confessed my sins to the Lord, and he has forgiven me. Some of you have probably already done the same. Those in category two who have never received Christ, if you haven't already accepted him today you need to do that tonight, don't wait until tomorrow. We do not have the assurance we will live until tomorrow. Tonight might be our last hours upon this earth, I urge you to make that decision now.

The gospel of John [John 1:12] said, "but as many as received him, to them gave he power to become sons [and daughters] of God, even to them that believe in his name. This is what you who have never received him need to do.

You that are in the category with the five foolish virgins need to follow the scripture in [I John 1:9], "if we confess our sins, he is faithful and just to forgive us our sins, and to cleanse us from all unrighteousness."

I am going to lead us in a prayer. If you will pray this prayer, and mean it in your heart you will be saved. First before we pray I would like to see the hands raised of all that would like to pray this prayer. Would you hold up your hand at this time? Praise God! I see that about everyone wants to pray this prayer. I usually like to see those that want to receive Christ make it publicly by coming down to the altar, but since there will not be enough room down front, I will ask you to pray where you are. Now repeat after me.

Dear Jesus, I realize I am a sinner.
I cannot do anything in myself to be saved.
I believe you died on the cross-for my sins.
I repent for the way I have been living.
I confess my sins before you tonight.
And I receive you into my heart, amen.

If you have been sincere in this prayer, you are no longer a sinner, but a sinner who has been saved by grace. Can you say hallelujah?

If I have counted right there has been over three hundred who have either rededicated their life to Christ or have been saved tonight. You that have been saved for the first time, we will be having a baptism service soon, and we strongly recommend you be baptized. Lets sing a course before we go, if you know it please help us sing.

"Thank you Lord for saving my soul, ----Thank you Lord, for making me whole, ----Thank you Lord for giving to me thy great salvation so rich and free."

God bless everyone as we go our separate ways; don't forget tomorrow morning at 9 o'clock a.m. we will be teaching on the same subject that we have taught tonight for those who were turned away tonight. If you have loved ones, or neighbors that are not here tonight, urge them to come at 9 o'clock a.m. tomorrow. You who were here tonight please come at 1 o'clock p.m. tomorrow, lets pray.

Father we come to you in the name of Jesus, thank you for the decisions, which have been made tonight. We pray that each one has grown close to you this night, and may the love of the father, son, and Holy Spirit abide with us forever. Amen."

It has been a long day for everyone, but no one seems to be in any hurry, they are hugging one another, and saying God bless you brother or sister. Everyone is on cloud nine, so they have forgotten it has been a long day.

Finally everyone begins to leave for home. Stan and Josie are talking on the way home what a difference this night has made in their lives. As soon as they get home they crash into bed exhausted, but happy.

Chapter 8

TIME OF REJOICING

Stan and Josie sleep late. When they get out of bed they get a shower, and get dressed for the day. Josie fixes breakfast, and they have a good breakfast, and watch the news and do their chores before going to the afternoon Bible study. The news is still all bad and no one seems to know yet just what has happened. They get their chores done around the house and leave for the afternoon Bible study.

Stan and Josie arrive at the church early for the study. They try to get a seat down close to the front. The church is soon filled. Deacon Bill comes to the podium and asks if everyone is ready for the study. They all answer, "Yes." Deacon Bill said, "I have mentioned being born again, I think it might be good tonight to study the "parable of the sower." I have heard only 25% of the people who go to church today are saved, and when I notice how some have been living I can believe it. I believe the Bible does teach we should lay off all the sins that so easy beset us and run with patience the race before us. Although the Bible does say we are "saved by grace," it also teaches us we should live a holy and righteous life. There are many things in the

New Testament, which teach living a holy life. We will only mention a couple at this time.

Turn to [Romans Chapter six] we will not read the entire Chapter but would like to read about three verses. You can read the rest later. Look at verses one and two, "what shall we say then? Shall we continue in sin, that grace may abound? God forbid. How shall we that are dead to sin, live any longer therein?" [verse 6].Knowing this, that our old man is crucified with him [Christ], that the body of sin might be destroyed, that henceforth we should not serve sin." One more verse, [verse 12] "let not sin therefore reign in your mortal body that ye should obey in the lust thereof." I have only mentioned about four verses you should read the rest. This is not saying that Christians never sin, but they are to grow in Christ. If you haven't grown in Christ since you received the word, you need to examine yourself to see if you are really a Christian. You can do this by looking into the mirror of God's word.

Now let's go to the parable of the sower in [Matthew Chapter 13:3-8]. "and he spoke to them in parables, saying, behold a sower went forth to sow; and when he sowed, some seeds fell by the way side, and the fowls came and devoured them: some fell upon stony places, where they had not much earth: and forthwith they spring up, because they had no deepness of earth: and when the sun was up, they were scorched; and because they had no root, they withered away. And some fell among thorns; and the thorns sprung up and choked them: but others fell into good ground, and brought forth fruit, some and hundredfold, some sixty-fold, some thirty fold." The disciples came and asked Jesus why he was teaching in parables. He said, "therefore I speak to them in parables: because they seeing see not, and hearing they hear not, neither do they understand." Then Jesus explains the parable in [verses 19-23]. Jesus spoke of the parables as being in four categories: The seed which fell by the wayside, the seed which fell in stony places, the seed which fell among thorns, and the seed which fell on good ground. Let's take the parable one category at a time.

Category one: seed that fell by the wayside "when any one heareth the word of the kingdom and understandeth it not, then cometh the wicked one, and catcheth away that which was sown in his heart, this is he which recieveth seed by the wayside." We notice the seed is the Word of God. These are the one who listen to the word and fail to understand. This is why we preachers should be careful to explain the Word of God in it fullness. We notice the seed falls on the wayside. This is soil, which isn't plowed. It is usually a path or road, which goes through the field. Hosea tells us to "sow to yourself in righteousness, reap in mercy; break up the fallow ground for it is time to seek the Lord." Notice the birds represent the wicked one, which as you know is the devil. I believe in every sermon the teacher or preacher teaching the word should always end up at the cross, and give the listeners the opportunity to receive Jesus, try to get the person to commit themselves by coming forward. Then the scripture can be explained to them more fully. One of the big mistakes we make, many times we pray for the person, we lead them in the sinners prayer then we tell them they are saved, but there is always the possibility the person praying didn't really understand what they are praying and they need to be nurtured by explaining the word to them more fully. If we do not do this the devil may snatch the seed from them as soon as they leave and we may never see them again. Of course there are those who come into our presents who are just coming to make someone happy and have no intention of coming again, but even then sometimes when the word is preached to them the Holy Spirit deals with them and

Revival Of Those Left Behind

they receive Christ, and then need to be nurtured by other Christians.

Now let's go to **category two:** the seed that fell on stony places. They receive the word with joy, because they have no root in themselves and because the word hasn't taken root when tribulation or persecution arises they are soon offended and fall away. We have no root in our self to be a Christian. The Bible teaches we are to be rooted and grounded in Christ. If we are to live a Christian life we must be in the vine and remain in the vine [Jesus]. Jesus said, [John 15:4, 5] "abide in me, and I in you. As the branch cannot bear fruit of itself, except it abide in the vine; no more can ye, except ye abide in me. I am the vine, ye are the branches: he that abides in me, and I in him, the same bringeth much fruit: for without me ye can do nothing." When we abide in Christ the Holy Spirit is living in us, and he will help us in any tribulation or persecution which may come against us if we will let him guide our lives in all circumstances, but if we try to do it on our own we fall on our face. It is necessary that we abide in Jesus. If we are not bearing fruit we should take a look in God's mirror, which is the word, and check to see if we are being fruitful, according to his word. If we are not being fruitful we may be like the seed that took no root. If this is the case we need to ask the seed sower to help us clear the stones in our garden, and to sow new seed.

Let's take up the **category three:** "he that received seed among the thorns is he that heareth the word; and the cares of world, and the deceitfulness of riches, choke the word, and he becometh unfruitful." I am sure you know some people who are in this category. They come to church sometime maybe Christmas or Easter but they let the cares of the world keep them from coming to church. They have bought so many recreation toys and fine things trying to keep up with others. They either have to be out playing with their toys or trying to keep up their property on the Lord's Day. They have worked all the week, sometimes husband and wife long hours to pay their Bills. When Sunday comes they can't go to church because they need some time to spend with the family. I know you have heard someone say those words. They don't realize what a better day it would be if they spent time in church with their family on Sunday. They might have less heartache later on in life. There is a saying "the families that prays together, stays together." This might not be true in every case, but polls taken, prove that family's who attend church are more apt to stay together. Then there are those who say they can't tithe because if they do they will not be able to pay their bills. What does the word say about this, it said [Malachi 3:10,11] "bring your tithes into the storehouse, that there may be meat in mine house, and prove me now herewith sayeth the Lord of host, if I will not open the windows of heaven, and pour out a blessing, that there shall not be room enough to receive it. And I will rebuke the devourer for your sake, and he shall not destroy the fruit of your ground; neither will your vine cast her fruit before the time in the field, saith the Lord of host." This scripture is talking about a farmer because in those days most people were farmers. If we were to apply it to our modern times it would apply to all kinds of workers, technicians, and business men. If we do what he said, we will work up to better paying jobs, and increase our business and make it more profitable. This sometimes takes faith and hard work. Sometimes we may be tried [like Job, the man in the book of Job] to see if we will be faithful. Paul said to Timothy, [II Timothy 3:12] "yea an all that will live Godly in Christ Jesus shall suffer persecution. James said in [James 1:12], blessed is the man that endureth temptation: for when he is tried, he shall receive the crown of life, which the Lord has promised to them that love him.

Now let's go to the deceitfulness of riches, which choke the word and they become unfruitful. If you will look around you in church there are very few which are rich. Jesus said, "It is harder for a camel to go through the eye of a needle than for a rich man to enter the kingdom." Jesus is not saying rich people cannot enter into heaven. He is saying it is harder for a camel to go thru the eye of a needle than a rich man to get into heaven. He is not saying a camel cannot go through the eye of a needle, but it is harder. We have heard the eye of a needle is a passage way where a camel has to have the burden unloaded from him, and the camel has to get down on his knees and crawl through. Jesus has just been talking to a wealthy person who had asked him what he would have to do to enter the kingdom. Jesus told him to keep the commandments. He said he had kept them all from his youth. Jesus knew he hadn't kept the commandments from his youth, so Jesus said if ye will be perfect sell what you have, give to the poor: and come follow me. The Bible said he went away sorrowful: for he had great possessions. The rich man could get to heaven, but he needed to be rich with his giving to the Lord's work, and get on his knees and humble himself before the Lord. Remember with God all things are possible. Many of the Old Testament patriarchs were rich, but they were made rich because they served and trusted God. The apostle Paul instructing Timothy [I Timothy 6:8-10] "and having food and raiment let us be their with content. But they that will be rich fall into temptation and a snare, and into many foolish and hurtful lusts, which drown men in destruction and perdition. For the love of money is the root of all evil: which some coveted after, they have erred from the faith, and pierced themselves through with many sorrows."

Lets go to **category four:** "but he that recieveth seed among the good ground is he who heareth the word, and understandeth it; which also beareth fruit, and bringeth forth, some an hundredfold, some sixty, some thirty. This is the category every pastor wishes his church was full of, but it isn't normally true. Although many churches have good workers, some of them are bringing forth a hundredfold, some sixty, and some thirty, but there are those attend church who never give any thought to inviting others to church, praying for the church, giving to expand the gospel, teaching, helping, cleaning, repairing, or any thing else that needs to be done. When we become a Christian we are compelled by Christ to take up our cross and follow him. We are only asked to be willing to exercise, whatever talent he has given to us. Not all Christians are called to do every job in the church. The Bible said we have different gifts and each Christian should use his gift to the best of his or her ability. I pray you are using your gift, if you are not there is weakness in the church.

We will end our study for this afternoon, but before we have our benediction we will give you an opportunity to come down front and pray. I do not know what your need is, but God knows. What ever you need, tell Him about it. If you feel the seed hasn't taken root in your life, open up your heart and allow him to sow more seed. If you haven't been using your talent or gift ask him to forgive you tonight.

Many people come down to pray. Stan and Josie are among those who come down. Although they had committed themselves to the Lord last night, they felt it would be good to go down front. Some are asking the Lord to come into their life; some are rededicating their life to the Lord. Deacon Bill leads them in the sinner's prayer, and a prayer of committal. Then he tells them to get into the word, and let God speak to them, and not to neglect to pray every day.

Josie notices everyone is much happier today than they were yesterday. Everyone is hugging one another, and saying; I love you brother or sister. Some are crying for joy. Josie sees Mary, Maria's sister. She goes over and gives her a big hug then they begin to talk about what a difference inviting Christ into their lives has made. They talk about how now they are going to take up their cross and follow Jesus, regardless of the cost. They talk about how they wish they had listened to Maria, when she would try to tell them Jesus was coming soon.

Josie said, "Just think if we had listened to Maria, we would be in heaven today with Maria's family, and with our own children, but it is good to know if we stay faithful until the end we will be able to go be with them very soon."

"I have never been a real emotional person," said Mary, "but tonight I feel like praising the Lord. I am sure the Holy Spirit has entered my life this night, and he is urging me to glorify the name of Jesus, and lift up his precious name."

"I feel the same way," said Josie.

By this time Stan and Paul say they are on cloud nine, they feel the same way the girls feel they notice the whole crowd seems to be filled with joy.

They notice Deacon Bill has both hands raised to the heaven, he is rejoicing, and praising the Lord. He is saying hallelujah, hallelujah, hallelujah, praise you Jesus, praise you father, praise you Holy Ghost.

Deacon Bill said I feel so good I think we should sing some of the old hymns. Lets all sing. Then he begins to sing the song "amazing grace how sweet the sound that saved a wretch like me, I was once lost but now I am found." Everyone joins in singing to the top of his or her voice.

Then he leads off with, "praise God, praise God, praise God, praise God, praise God, praise God, praise God, praise God."

Then he leads off with; "oh how I love Jesus, oh how I love Jesus, oh how I love Jesus, because he first loved me."

Then he leads off with; "I am so wondrously saved from sin, Jesus so sweetly abides within, down at the cross where he took me in, glory to his name, glory to his name------ glory to his name----- there to my heart was the blood applied, glory to his name." Every one has their hands raised to heaven by this time, and is praising God.

Stan whispers and said, "I didn't know you could have such a good time like this at church. I have had fun at the ball game when our team was winning, but I have never felt this much joy."

When everyone begins to come down off of cloud nine, Deacon Bills said, "this has been a glorious afternoon. We will not have a benediction on this service come back tonight and bring this sweet spirit with you. We will meet at 7: o'clock. If God is willing, and he doesn't change my mind we will study, "the signs of his coming". Good afternoon, and don't be late.

Stan and Josie leave for home. Josie said to Stan, "I can't believe we feel so good today, when we felt so bad yesterday when we realized our children were missing. Jesus sure has made a difference in our lives and the way we feel".

"Yes, He sure has," said Stan, "I have read where when a person gets saved the Holy Spirit comes into their lives and makes them a new person, then the Holy Spirit takes up residence in their life to lead and guide their life in Holy living, and is a comforter to them. I believe He is comforting us this day with the assurance we will be going to be with our children soon. Our children are there with Jesus today. I do not know if they can see us, but if they can, I believe they are rejoicing about us becoming a Christian, and saying mom, dad we will see you in a few days."

Revival Of Those Left Behind

When Stan and Josie arrive home, as soon as they pull into their driveway some of the neighbors come right over. They wanted to know if Stan and Josie had found out what had happened to all their loved ones who were missing. The people, which came over, were the Mcelliot's. They had been neighbors of Stan and Josie for a number of years, their children had gone to school with Stan and Josie's children. They had been good neighbors, but had never wanted to go to church. They thought as long as you were a good person that was all that mattered. Stan and Josie invite them into the house. Josie could hardly wait to tell them what had happened to them that day. She said, "Yes we know where our loved ones are gone, and we know where they are tonight, Jesus has come in the rapture and taken all the true Christians to be with Him in heaven. We received Jesus into our hearts, and soon we are going to be with them. We are comforted tonight in the Holy Spirit, hallelujah; praise the wonderful name of Jesus."

"But wait," said Mr. Mcelliot, "you guys have been going to church almost every Sunday. Now tell us why you guys aren't gone to heaven with them."

"Ok," said Stan, "I will answer your question. True we have been regular every Sunday, unless there was a ball game or some other pleasure event taking place. Then we ditched church and went to those. But we have found out the truth. We have been going to a very liberal church, which didn't teach the gospel. We had thought if we went to church, that made us a Christian, but we have found out today that there is more to being a Christian than just attending church. We knew about Jesus, and believed he had died on the cross-for our sins, and we had been baptized, but we never had invited Jesus into our lives. This afternoon after the Bible study we confessed to Christ our sins, and accepted him into our lives. When we did this, something happened. We received the assurance that our children were with Jesus and we would soon be with them."

"But I don't understand," said Mr. Mcelliot. "we have always been good, we have tried to be good to others, we don't drink to excess, we don't use bad language, sometimes we gave to those in need, but we didn't believe in going to church, the churches are just out to get peoples money. I don't know why we got left behind we have been as good as a lot of Christians I know."

"Yes," said Stan, "I am sure you guys have been as good as many Christians, we thought the same thing, but we have found out, being good is not what saves a person. The Bible says," There is none that doeth good, no not one." James one of the New Testament writers said; "for whosoever shall keep the whole law, and offend in one point, he is guilty of all" Paul said in Romans, "all have sinned and come short of the glory of God". So that makes us all sinners. Then Paul also said in Romans; "the wages of sin is death, but the gift of God is eternal life, through Jesus our Lord. Paul also wrote; "for by grace are we saved, thru faith, and that not of yourselves, it is a gift of God; not of works less any man should boast." In the gospel of John Jesus said, "God so loved the world that he gave his only begotten son that whosoever believeth in him should not perish, but have eternal life." What this verse in John is talking about is, God sent his son [Jesus] into this world as a baby to grow up to be a man, to teach and to heal the sick, raise the dead, and many other things to prove he was God's son. Then he died on the cross-for the sins of the whole world. It wasn't the Jewish people who condemned him, nor was it the roman soldiers who executed him that was responsible for his death, but my sins and your sins. He died that you and I might have life, and have it more abundantly. So now we do not have to die for our sins, but realize we are a sinner, repent and confess we are a sinner, believe he died on the cross-for our sins, and invite him into our hearts. He then will come into our hearts, and make us a new person. His spirit will then take up his abode in our life and to teach, and guide us in all ways of truth and right, and give us comfort in days like these. We are comforted tonight to know we can also go to heaven to be with Jesus. We realize the days ahead are not going to be easy. We will have to stand against the antichrist, and not worship him, or take his mark. We know this will lead to us not being able to buy or sell, or even get a job, and also we will be killed. We are determined that from here on we will take up our cross and follow Jesus, and by the power given to us through the Holy Spirit we shall stand for Jesus."

Mr. Mcelliot want's to know if he can accept Christ like they have. "Sure," said Stan. "We are going to Bible study again at 7:00 tonight. You guys can go with us. I believe this would be a way of saying to Jesus; you guys really mean business with him.

"Sure" said Mr. and Mrs. Mcelliot, "we will be happy to go with you."

"Ok," said Stan "we will leave about 6:15 tonight, we want to be on time."

"Ok," said the Mcelliots. "See you tonight."

They leave for home. Stan and Josie are very tired, so they crash in their lounge chairs to rest.

Chapter 9

"SIGNS OF HIS COMING"

S tan and Josie arrive at the church early. They have also brought the Mcelliots with them. There is already a long line of people to get into the church.

"I am sure glad we came early," said Josie, "if we had come any later we may have not gotten in. There are many people in line, I didn't see this afternoon."

When they got in line they found out many of the people standing in line had been there for the afternoon study, but was unable to get in because of the crowd. They had been waiting in line since the afternoon study. When Stan, Josie and the Mcelliots finally get inside they discovered the church was almost full. Soon the ushers had to close the doors so as not to violate the fire codes, but some of the men had set up a monitor outside so people could sit on the lawn and hear and watch the study. It wasn't long until one of the ushers came and informed Deacon Bill that there were 2 or 3 hundred people gathered outside.

Deacon Bill came to the podium and welcomed everyone to the study. He said he was happy so many had come and those outside would be able to hear because of the monitors which had been set up. He said, "I have been reminded today of the multitude which gathered on the mountainside in Jesus' day to listen to Jesus. I don't think you have gathered here tonight to listen to me, but to listen to Jesus through his word. I announced this afternoon we would speak tonight on "the signs of his coming". We spoke yesterday afternoon about those being left behind. We had put the ones left behind in three categories. Category one was the five foolish virgins, category two was those who had gone to church but never had accepted Christ. Then the third category was those, which had hardened their heart toward the word. We are not going to repeat that study tonight, although we did repeat it in the morning study. You may say this afternoon why is he studying about the signs of his coming if he [Jesus] has already come. The reason is to show us that the prophets did warn us that Jesus was coming, and gave us signs to teach us He was coming. The apostle Paul has said in [I Thessalonians 5:1-6,] "but of the times and the seasons, brethren, you have no need that I write unto you. For yourself know perfectly that the day of the Lord so cometh as a thief in the night. For when they shall say peace and safety; then sudden destruction cometh upon them, as travail upon a woman with child; and they shall not escape. But ye brethren are not in darkness, that the day should overtake you as a thief." This was a continuation of the things Paul had said in Chapter 4 where he had spoke about the Lord coming in the rapture. When I read this it reminded me of how we awoke yesterday morning to find many of our loved ones were missing. Let us go ahead now and read [verse 5 and 6,] "ye are all the children of light, and the children of the day; we are not of the night, nor of darkness. Therefore let us not sleep, as others do; but let us watch and be sober." This reminds me of the ten virgins in Matthew Chapter 25. Where the five foolish virgins had not watched, and had gotten left behind.

Ok, lets talk about, The Signs of His Coming. I will mention **"six signs of His coming."**

Sign number 1: Rebirth of Israel:

Turn to [Jeremiah 23:7, 8.] "therefore behold, the days come, saith the Lord, that they shall no more say, the Lord liveth, which brought the children of Israel out of the land of Egypt; but the Lord liveth which brought up and which lead the seed of the house of Israel out of the north country, and from all the countries whither I have driven them; and they shall dwell in their own land." Israel had been driven out of their nation in A.D. 70 by Titus and his Roman armies. The Jews settled in other countries throughout the world. It was a dream of many of them to be able to return to their land and be a nation again. Some of them were already moving to their land, which was the land of Palestine. On May 14th 1948, the United Nations voted to let Israel become a nation again. At that time they begin to return to their homeland by the thousands. Their becoming a nation again hasn't been without hardship. The day the United Nations allowed them to become a nation again, a war broke out with the Arab nations, and there has been war ever since. Perhaps this is what Jesus is talking about when he said you will hear of wars and rumors of wars in Matthew Chapter 24. A few years ago I asked a Jewish guide by the name of Jacob who had returned to the land of Israel from Argentina, which was a peaceful nation, why he had come back to Israel, why he had moved to a land which was experiencing so much turmoil." He said to me, "God put it in my heart to return to the land of my fathers."

The prophet Ezekiel has prophesied God will bring Israel from the heathen lands and make them one nation again. When they became one nation, they became as the nation of Israel, instead of two nations Judah and Israel. If you have studied in the Old Testament about King Solomon and his son Jeroboam, because of Solomon's sins the nation of Israel was divided into two nations Judah and Israel. The capital city Jerusalem was in the nation of Judah consisting of two tribes Judah, and Benjamin. The other ten tribes made up the northern kingdom, which was Israel. Today the Jews are back in their own land, and they are there to stay!

Sign number 2: Social unrest

Turn to [II Timothy 3:1, 2] this is the Apostle Paul speaking again. "This know also, that in the last days perilous times shall come, for men shall be lovers of their own selves, covetous, boasters, proud, blasphemers, and disobedient to parents, unthankful, unholy." Paul mentions several other things in the next three chapters, but we will not read them at this time. I don't think it is really much use to even comment on these eight things Paul has spoken about. We will hit them lightly. I think you understand we are living in perilous times today. So many things are taking place around the world. People are losing their jobs, their wealth, their homes, their families, and many other things. It has a lot to do with people being lovers of their own selves, they are not content with what God has given them, and they are coveting riches through the wrong channels. They are saying if I could hit the jackpot, or if I could win the lottery I would be happy. Wrong! Money doesn't bring happiness. The Bible said, "Godliness with contentment brings great gain." So if you want to have it made, turn your life over to God. Sometimes people go around boasting about the things they have done and what a smart person they are. The truth is, without God we are nothing. Some go around with their head in the air as if everything they are is because of who they are. Wrong! It is who we are in Jesus! Without him we would be nothing.

I think it is blasphemy to God the way we live. Children are disobedient to parents like never before. I do not believe it is always the children's fault. I believe we as parents have failed to raise our children the Bible way. Then there are many parents who have gone awol. They are neglecting their children, so as to have a little fun. Satan is behind all of it. He is out to destroy as many families as he can. God has told us in the Bible how to correct our children, and we are to bring them up in the nurture and admonition of the Lord. This is not happening today, parents are trying to give them everything, helping them get a good education so they can get a good job, but they don't seem to realize how hard some of their families have worked, and sacrifice for them. Next is unholy. Churches use to preach holiness, but you don't hear much of this preached anymore. Most of the preachers have been preaching a watered down version of the Bible,

Sign number 3, religious apostasy:

We have already said some of the preachers have quit preaching holiness, they say they are afraid to preach the truth in fear of causing their members to leave the church, but I suppose if the facts are known they have grown up in a very liberal world. They have gotten used to being liberal and don't know the different. Some of them have been educated in liberal universities, and seminaries who don't take the Bible as the infallible word of God. Some of the professors don't believe in a virgin birth, they don't believe in holiness. The apostle Paul spoke to Timothy about the last days, he said, [II Timothy 3:7] there would be those that would be "ever learning, and never able to come to the truth.

Now as Jannes and Jamborees withstood Moses so do these also resist the truth; men of corrupt minds reprobate concerning the truth." Here is a way you can tell if your Pastor has been preaching the truth. Does he ever preach on sin? Does he ever mention the Ten Commandments? Does he teach God is to be first in our lives? Does he teach you should honor your father and mother? Does he ever teach it is wrong to covet? Does he teach it's wrong to have sex out of marriage? Does he teach you should set aside one day a week for worship and rest? Does he teach it is wrong to steal? Does he teach it is not a wise thing to drink? Does he say anything about loving your neighbors? What about bearing false witness?

Now I know some of you are going to say, "Deacon Bill is teaching the old testament" I say to you, you don't know your Bible. Let us look in the new testament what Jesus' said, [Matthew 17:17,18,19,20,] "think not I am come to destroy the law, or the prophets: I am not come to destroy, but fulfill, for verily I say unto you till heaven and earth pass, one jot or title shall in no wise pass from the law, till all be fulfilled. Whosoever therefore shall break one of these least of commandments, and shall teach men so, he shall be called least in the kingdom of heaven: but whosoever shall do and teach them, shall be called great in the kingdom of heaven. For I say unto you, that except your righteousness shall exceed the righteousness of the scribes and Pharisees, ye shall in no case enter the kingdom of heaven." God goes on in this Chapter and expounds on some of these commandments. Maybe you should read it when you get home if you don't believe it. What God has said about holiness? God has said in the old and the new testaments, "be ye holy as I am holy". Thank God some of our churches are still preaching the word of God. Many are gone to heaven because they believed the word, and kept it.

I think it is getting about time to end our study for tonight; we will come back tomorrow night at seven o'clock and continue our study. We will study political unrest, social promiscuity, and natural disaster then. We have been asked by the city officials to not have a daytime service, so everyone will return to their jobs. Some of the men will set up some temporary lights on the lawn area for those which can not get into the building. It would be a good idea to bring you a lawn chair tomorrow night, and a coat in case the night air is cool. Parking could be a problem, so I urge you to carpool, there is a shopping center down the street, and maybe some of you that have vans might think about running shuttles from the shopping center. We will be taping the study tomorrow night if anyone happens to miss you can pick up a tape later.

I would be very wrong to close out this tonight without giving an alter call for you to receive Christ. If the church you have been attending hasn't been preaching the gospel, of "Jesus Christ dying on the cross for our sins," and you haven't come to the place in your life, where you have realized you were a sinner, and haven't come to repentance, received Jesus into your heart as your Lord and Savior, we want to invite you to do this tonight. I think there is too many people here tonight which haven't received Jesus, to invite you to come forward to the altar, so we will not ask you to come down front. If you haven't received Jesus we invite you to stand at this time. You that are outside watching the monitors are invited to do the same. We are going to say a prayer inviting Jesus into our heart. I will ask you to repeat the prayer after me:

Dear Jesus, I confess I am a sinner,

I believe you died on the cross-to pay the penalty for my sins. I realize if you hadn't died on the cross there would be no forgiveness for sin. I would be doomed to spend eternity in hell. I believe your word if I will accept you into my heart I can live with you in heaven. I receive you into my heart today and I thank you for coming into my life, amen. If you prayed this prayer, and believed it in your heart you have been saved. Now you need to let the Holy Spirit begin to rule and reign in your life. Before we leave lets sing a song of thanksgiving:

"Thank you Lord for saving my soul,

Thank you Lord for making me whole,

Thank you Lord for giving to me, thou great salvation so rich and free."

Now just raise your hands and just praise him." Every hand is lifted high. People are praising God with all their heart. Some are apologizing to others for wronging them in the past. People are hugging one another never has there been love in the church like there is tonight. Revival is taking place at Agape Church.

When everything begins to settle down Deacon Bill said, "God bless everyone, and we will see you tomorrow night."

The Mcelliot's are still hugging Stan and Josie and telling them how much they appreciate that they have invited them to the study. Mr. Mcelliot said, "I never knew until today the importance of inviting Jesus into my heart. I had always thought that I was good enough, and could make it on my own. I had told my wife and children it was foolish to attend church. We were teaching our children the same thing. We wanted them to have a good education, excel in sports, have fun and not worry about going to church to learn about Christ. I realize today just how wrong I was. I am glad our children were caught out to be with Jesus before they grew up believing just like dad. I miss them very much, but I am comforted today knowing they are with Jesus, and since I have invited Jesus into my heart I will be able to go be with them".

Stan and Josie tells them although they went to church on Sunday, they had never invited Christ to be their savior until they begin to study with Deacon Bill. They have the same comfort as the Mcelliots.

The Mcelliots both talk about how they were brought up in church as a child. Mr. Mcelliot said, "I had gotten my eyes on man instead of God, I had seen too many people, which were testifying to be Christians, but were not walking the talk. There was this one preacher which everyone had respected. He got caught making love to one of the members. This was the last straw for me, I quit going to church, and said I could live for God at home. But I didn't. I was more interested in the good life for my family and me. Of course I didn't really know the devil was blinding me to reality. One other thing I realize now is preachers are not perfect, and they are not exempt from the temptations of the devil. God expects me to live for him as same as preachers."

When they went out of the church to go home the news media was outside the door interviewing everyone about what was taking place. They couldn't believe the joy everyone was expressing, and people were telling them Jesus had changed their lives, and how they would be going to heaven to be with their families soon. The news reporter is asking, "Who is teaching the class if the Pastor is missing?" Someone tells him it is one of the deacons of the church that had gotten left behind, and his name is Bill. He asked if someone would please let him know when Deacon Bill comes out of the church. Soon someone said Deacon Bill is coming out. The news reporter rushes over to meet him. He asked Deacon Bill if he can interview him about the Bible studies they are having.

"I am really sorry," said Deacon Bill, I am really tired this evening, but will meet with you sometime tomorrow."

"Good said the reporter, would eight o'clock tomorrow morning be a good time for you."

"Sure," said Deacon Bill, "that will be fine; we will be meeting again at seven o'clock tomorrow night feel free to come to the services."

Stan, Josie and the Mcelliots rejoiced all the way home. Josie said; "it would seem impossible for people whose loved ones had disappeared the day before could have such joy, but when Jesus and the Holy Spirit comes into our lives it gives us joy to know there is going to be a reunion in heaven. It is like every one is headed for home, some are ready for the first flight out, and they are packed up and ready to go. There are others who want to go, but they don't have their baggage in order, and they are left behind, but they are determining to be on the next flight out. I think we are all determined to be on the next flight regardless of the cost."

They arrive home. The Mcelliots say, "We will see you tomorrow." They give Stan and Josie a big hug, and depart for their house. Stan and Josie go into their house.

Stan and Josie begin to relax in their favorite chairs. After relaxing for a while, Josie goes into the kitchen to prepare a snack. Stan turns on the TV. to see what might be happening on the news. The reporter is still talking about there still being a lot of things, which are happening throughout the world.

He said, "Emergency crews are still very busy trying to take care of all the accidents which had occurred yesterday morning. The military is having total confusion, and defeat in many places. The top General has reported they were not prepared for what ever has taken place. The news reporter said if we didn't have enough problems there are riots breaking out in some of the larger cities. People are breaking into stores, and looting.

A police spokesman said; many of their officers haven't reported in at all in the past two days and it is assumed they are missing with the other people who are missing. People are jamming their lines wanting to know if they are doing anything to find the missing. He said we can assure you we are doing the best we can, and soon as we find them we will let you know.

They are asking everyone to please not call 911 unless you have an emergency, and said, we must try to keep our lines open for an emergency.

The reporter said, many people are blaming the radical Christians for what has been taking place. We have been checking on some of the churches around town. After a break we will take you to the Agape Church where we had a live report earlier this afternoon."

Stan calls Josie in from the kitchen to hear the live report.

After a commercial break the reporter comes back, and said, "Before I take you to the Agape Church, I would like to take you out to the Ladoci church. There is as much difference in these churches today as there is in daylight and dark. At the Ladoci church people are weeping and are in a bad mood. They are still questioning where their loved ones are gone. Some of them are angry with Pastor Joe for leading them astray. Pastor Joe is assuring them that they will soon find out where their loved ones are. He is assuring them it is not the rapture, as some are saying. He said he thinks some of these radical Christians may be responsible.

Ok now let's go over to Agape Church and see the difference. As we were there live today. One of the deacons that said he got left behind because of sin in his life was teaching a Bible study and the church was filled to capacity, with about three hundred people. They had monitors set up outside on the lawn with another three or four hundred. At the end Deacon Bill gave an invitation for people to accept

Christ. When he had them to repeat a prayer, about every one was praying the prayer. Some of them told us later, they had already prayed the prayer, but was saying the prayer again along with those who were saying the prayer for the first time to help them in their praying. After the prayer they sang a song of thanks, I have never seen such love and joy in a church, everyone were hugging each other and praising God. After the study I interviewed several of the people. I told them I couldn't understand how they could be so happy the day after their love ones had disappeared. They told me it was the Holy Spirit which had entered them, and was giving them comfort, and assurance they would be reunited with their loved ones in heaven soon. I had a short interview with Deacon Bill when he came out. He was very tired, but agreed to meet with me tomorrow morning at eight o'clock. We will interview Deacon Bill and Pastor Joe at the same time in the studio. So be sure to tune in tomorrow morning at eight o'clock. We will take a station break at this time, when we come back we will have the weather and other news. There hasn't been any sports' taking place today."

Stan and Josie turn off the TV, have a snack and relax before retiring for the night.

Chapter 10

NEW DEVELOPMENTS ON THE HORIZON

Stan and Josie wake up after a good night's sleep having assurance their children are in Heaven. Josie said to Stan, "it sure is quite around here without the children".

"Yes," said Stan, "I miss them coming in our room and jumping in the bed with us."

"Yes," said Josie, "I remember two days ago waking up early and finding our children gone. When I first woke up this morning I listened for them in their room, and thought they were there. Then I remembered what had really taken place they were gone to be with Jesus. I still miss them very much, but it makes me feel better to know they are there with Jesus, and soon we will be with Jesus and be reunited with them."

"Yes," said Stan, "I am glad we decided to go over to the Agape Church two days ago. If we had not gone there we would never have met such a wonderful man and teacher like Deacon Bill. He may not call himself a preacher, but he sure makes a good teacher. I wouldn't mind having him as our Pastor."

"Yes for sure," said Josie, "if he had been our Pastor we would have gone with our children in the rapture. Maria tried to get us to come to hear their Pastor, but I thought he was a little on the radical side, but now I know different, he was concerned about the members of his church, and wanted them to be ready when Jesus' came, but it is good to know we will see them again if we are faithful."

Stan said, "yes, and I intend on being faithful from now on."

"Me to," said Maria.

Stan said, "I don't feel right about working at a casino, I have watched people who were on welfare spend their last dime gambling, and not have food on the table for their children. People, who gamble think they are going to win lots of money and sometimes some of the people do win, but over time they lose more than they win. They never think about if they win someone has to lose, and most of the time it is someone who needs their money for bills and food for their family. I have read in the Bible where we are not to covet anything that belongs to our neighbor, in fact it is one of the Ten Commandments. I feel it has been wrong for me to work in a casino, so today I am going to resign and find me another job."

"Yes", said Josie, "I feel the same way as you do. I have watched retired people that are on a fixed income pulling the slots and losing their money. Many of them look very sad about losing. I suppose Satan has made them think they are going to win, but most of the time that is not what happens. People do not understand the casino owners are the ones who are getting all of the money, building fine hotels and casino's that cost lots of money and they are not building them to give away money, but to make money. I am like you I am going to resign; I don't think Jesus want's me working there. I know he will provide a better job. I will fix us some breakfast, after breakfast we can call the boss at the casino.

"Ok" said Stan, "I will shave while you are preparing breakfast."

Soon Josie calls to Stan and tells him breakfast is ready. When he comes in the kitchen she said, "I hope you don't mind having oatmeal for breakfast, we are having oatmeal with raisins and walnuts."

"Sounds good to me," said Stan, "my cholesterol probably could use some oatmeal."

Stan turns on the TV and sets down for breakfast

The reporter is saying, "It is almost unbelievable what has been going on the past two days. People awoke two days ago with sirens, noise from accidents and explosions.

Then at the more liberal churches the Pastors are still preaching the same gospel which they have always preached, many of their members are almost in panic, acting like they have no hope whatsoever. Some of them are accusing their Pastor of preaching a false doctrine, and are going over to the other churches that are having revival. We were at the Agape Church last night and taped their study. Their Pastor had gone out in the rapture, but one of their deacons that had gotten left behind because of sin in his life was teaching the word. Several people responded to his invitation last night. He reported several hundred have given their life to Christ in the past two days.

Last night so many people came to the study the police had to come out and turn many away because the crowd was so large there wasn't any space left on their property. The church was full, the lawn was full with people watching monitors, and some were even sitting in the parking lot. The parking lot was full of cars; people were parking everywhere they could on the streets around the church.

Some were shuttling people from the shopping center a few blocks away.

After the service everything seemed to run pretty smooth, as far as traffic was concerned. Most of the people didn't seem to be in any hurry. They were courteous with each other and left a few at a time. The Agape Church wasn't the only church around town that was having revival, but happens to be the one we were interviewing. They seem to be having the largest crowds, we don't know why, but it could be Deacon Bill is a very good speaker, and seems to know what he is talking about.

The Mayor has asked Deacon Bill to use the football stadium tomorrow night for his teaching, and he has agreed to do so. The study will be tonight at seven o'clock at the agape church. He has invited Pastors and people from other churches to attend. We will be taping the service tonight for those who cannot attend because of work, and those who are in the hospitals, and rest homes.

Our hospitals are still very crowded from the accidents which happened two days ago. Both the hospitals and the rest homes are very short on staff. They are pleading with everyone if you are a doctor or a nurse please report to work today. Also if you are a doctor, or nurse that is retired, or just not working please come to work for a few days. They also have a shortage of maintenance people, technicians, housekeepers, and other positions. Please help if you can. The Mayor is also asking other people that work at other places to please return to work today.

We will be interviewing Deacon Bill from the Agape Church, and Pastor Joe from the Ladoci church at eight o'clock. They are two people with different opinions, so be sure to stay tuned. We are going to go now to our Washington newsroom, with Tom Brown."

"Good morning this is your reporter Tom Brown coming to you from Washington DC. We still have a lot of bad news people are still being reported dead from everything that took place two days ago. The hospitals are crowded, and there is a shortage of help, the elderly in the convalescent homes are dying because there is such a shortage of help they are not getting the needed medical help. The morgues are full of bodies waiting for burial. The airports are still trying to get everything cleaned up and repaired. Most of the runways have damage where planes have crashed and burned. Our airports are still crowded with people either waiting for their loved ones to arrive or they are waiting to board a plane to go home to be with their loved ones. Some planes are beginning to arrive, and take off, but very limited. Our freeways and interstates that are open are still reported to be very crowded. Many of them are still closed because of accidents that are still being cleared up from two days ago, also many are still closed because of damage that occurred because of accidents and explosions that took place two days ago when their drivers were suddenly missing from their cars. The railroads are still paralyzed while the limited amount of crews try to clean up the mess of twisted steel from the tracks where the trains have wrecked because of different things, some of the trains failed to take sidings, and had crashed into oncoming trains. Many of the tracks are going to have to be rebuilt. But in spite of all of this, that is happening, we seem to have good news going on around the world.

People are turning to Christ all over the world. Many people are reported of accepting Christ. Many churches are filled with people, and having to turn others away. People are going to these churches sad, and coming away rejoicing. They believe Jesus has taken their loved ones to be with him in Heaven, and he is going to send for them soon. On the other hand some of the Church Pastors are saying these people have a false hope, and Jesus hasn't come for anyone. But I believe something has lifted the spirits of those who believe Jesus has come for their loved ones.

I am thinking about going to church and study the Bible with them, some of my family is missing and I would like to investigate to see if they have really gone to Heaven, and if there is a way I can go be with them. I was brought up in church by my parents. They were believers, and I became a believer for a while, but after I graduated from college, and began to be successful in the world I drifted away from Christ. My children and parent's are missing. I am beginning to believe what some of these people are saying about the rapture. At this time we would like to go to a spokesman for the military, he seems to have some good news for us. Here is General Lee Hall."

"Good morning, I am General Hall; I would like to bring you up to date on some of the happenings in the Middle East. As we have reported in the past two days our military has been in chaos, many of our troops have vanished. It has left those which remain fighting with everything they have, but they have been so short handed they have been losing the battle; some have been taken prisoners by the enemy. Many of our helicopters have crashed, or have been shot down, many tanks have been blown up by the enemy. It has looked like we were going to have to surrender, but a new hope has come on the horizon.

There is a person by the name of Bar-Jesus who supposedly was dead, which has come back to life, and has been completely healed. The United Nations, Israel, and the Arab nations have hailed him as a great man. They say he is a great leader, and can bring peace to the world. He is meeting with the leaders of the United Nations at this time to work out the plans for a truce throughout the world.

Pastor R.B. McCartney

There has been a short truce at the present time while they work out the plans for a complete truce. A spokesman for the white house said; "it may be what we have been looking for, but will take a little time to work out all the plans." We will inform you later on what develops, but this looks like the greatest news we have had for a long time."

"Thank you General Lee. Well folks you have heard General Lee's report. It sounds like good news to the world, and I am sure if you have loved ones in the military it is good news to you. Maybe our boys and girls will get to come home soon. We will give you back over to your local station."

"Thanks Tom Brown. We are going to take a station break. When we come back we will interview Pastor Joe and Deacon Bill from two of our local churches."

"All right we have here Pastor Joe, and Deacon Bill. We will start our interview with Deacon Bill since his church seems to be in revival. Deacon Bill first I would like to ask you, how much seminary training do you have?"

"Well Ann, I don't really have any seminary training. I have been studying the Bible for several years, and have been listening to our Pastor preach the word for about ten years. I don't consider myself to be a great teacher, or a preacher, but am being obedient to the commands of Jesus. Jesus said; in Matthew Chapter 28, and verse 19 "go ye therefore, and teach all nations, baptizing them in the name of the father, and of the son, and of the Holy Ghost." I believe he was talking to all Christians. In our church in the absence of the Pastor the Deacon is supposed to take over and give the word. This is what I have been doing."

"Ok Deacon Bill, thank you. Now let's go to Pastor Joe. Pastor Joe you are one of our outstanding Pastors here in the city. We would like to ask you the same question we have asked Deacon Bill. How much seminary training do you have?

"Well Ann I have a masters degree in a couple of different fields. I am studying for my doctorate degree at the present time; I hope to get it soon. I have had exclusive seminary training. I go to several church conferences on church growth every year. I believe I am one of the best qualified preachers in our town."

"Ok, thank you Pastor Joe. Now let's go back to Deacon Bill. Deacon Bill, where do you think the millions of people who are missing around the world have gone?"

"I believe beyond a shadow of doubt they are gone in the rapture."

Pastor Joe interrupts and says, "Where do you come up with this word rapture? It isn't even in the Bible."

"Ok," said Deacon Bill, "I will try to answer your question. In his first letter to the Thessalonians, the apostle Paul spoke about Jesus coming in the air. The dead in Christ would rise first, then the Christians who were in Christ would be caught up together in the clouds to meet the Lord in the air, and so would they ever be with the Lord. When we look up the word rapture it means caught up or caught out. This is what we are talking about."

"Ok," said Pastor Joe, "if Jesus has come for the Christians, why were you left behind?"

"That is easy to explain," said Deacon Bill, "I was letting sin rule me, I was living for myself to satisfy the lust of my flesh. Paul spoke these words in his letter to the Romans [Chapter 6:13] "let not sin reign in your mortal body, that you should obey it in the lust thereof"

"Wait," said Pastor Joe, "are you trying to tell us we are saved by works, instead of grace?"

"Not at all," said Deacon Bill.

"Hold everything," said Ann, "let me ask the questions. I want to ask Pastor Joe the same question I have asked you. Pastor Joe where do you think the people have all gone?"

"I am not sure," said Pastor Joe, "but I think these Pastors who are missing might be responsible. I am sure the Lord hasn't come. I believe we are saved by grace and not of works. I believe in Jesus, but I don't think it matters how we live as long as we believe."

"Ok," said Ann, "it seem like I have heard someone say the devil believes, does that make him a Christian?"

"No of course not," said Pastor Joe," I am not sure if what you have said about the devil is even in the Bible, sometimes people quote things out of context."

"Ok very well," said Ann, "but tell me why the people over at your church seem to be very sad, and still looking for answers, while over at the Agape Church where Deacon Bill is teaching they seem to be happy."

"I think Deacon Bill is giving them a false hope, and teaching things that are not in the Bible."

"Hold it right there, said Deacon Bill, let me explain one thing to you. I have been teaching from the Bible and only from the Bible. The people have been responding to the word, repenting of their sins and asking Christ to forgive them. Christ is doing what he said he would do, forgive them, the Holy Spirit is giving them comfort over the loss of their loved ones who have gone to be with Jesus."

"Ok," said Ann "lets move on to the next question. Since Pastor Joe has brought it up we will ask him this question first. Pastor Joe will you explain to us about this saved by grace, and not of works."

"Good" said Pastor Joe, "I will give you scripture on this one, we are going to turn to the book of Ephesians [Chapter 2, verses 8,and 9;] "for by grace are you saved through faith; and that not of yourselves; it is the gift of God; not of works lest any man should boast." If we take this just as Paul states it, we are saved by grace, and works has nothing to do with it. It doesn't make any difference how we live if we accept the grace of God."

"Good," said Ann, "now Deacon Bill, what do you have to say about grace, and works"

"Thanks," said Deacon Bill, "I will give you what the Bible has to say. I believe the scripture Pastor Joe has quoted. We are saved by grace, and not of works, but works is a by product of having been saved. Now I will go into detail. We cannot stop at the ninth verse; we must go on to the tenth verse. "For we are his workmanship created in Christ Jesus unto good works, which God hath before ordained that we should walk in them." Take note we are God's workmanship, created in Christ Jesus. When we come to Christ believe, repent, accept, and confess we become a new person. Jesus told Nicodemus in the Gospel of John, "Ye must be born again". Paul said to the Church at Corinth in [II Corinthians 5:17] "therefore if any man be in Christ, he is a new creation, old things are passed away; behold all things have become new." Now lets go back to the letter to the Ephesians [Chapter 4:22-24], "that ye put off concerning the former conversation the old man, which is corrupt according to the deceitful lusts; and be renewed in the spirit of your mind; and that ye put on the new man which after God is created in righteousness and true holiness."

We notice here in these scriptures he is talking about a new man, which is created in righteousness and true holiness. I am not going to read the rest of this Chapter, but I would urge you to read it. It mentions several things, which we as Christians should put off. I would also urge you to read Chapter five. It tells us we should be followers of Christ, and mentions several sins we shouldn't commit. Paul has taught holy living for Christians in all of his letters. Now you are probably thinking Deacon Bill thinks he is perfect. No! No! I am not saying I am perfect, I am not saying Christians are perfect.

I am saying when the Holy Spirit comes into our life he begins to work a new work in us to change us from the old sinful nature which we had, into something better. The Bible teaches us we are to be like Christ. I do not want to say to you I never sin. If there had not been un-confessed sin in my life I wouldn't be here today. I would be in Heaven with my family."

"Wait," said Pastor Joe, "you are speaking with a forked tongue, you are saying out of one side of your mouth Christians are perfect, and out of the other side Christians sin."

"I am sorry," said Deacon Bill, "I didn't mean for it to sound that way. The Bible said there is none righteous, no not one. The apostle John wrote in [I John 2:1] "my little children, these things I write unto you, that you sin not, and if any man sin, we have an advocate with the father, Jesus Christ the righteous." We have what Paul explains as a flesh nature and a spiritual nature. He said there is a war going on within us. The flesh is lusting against the spirit, and we cannot do the things we should. I heard an illustration given on this by a preacher once. He said the war between the flesh and the spirit is like two dogs in a fight. "Which one you say sic-hem, is the one that will win.

This might be a crude illustration, but I suppose it could be true. Let us turn to what the scripture has to say. Turn to [Galatians 5:16-25]. "This I say then, walk in the spirit, and ye shall not fulfill the lust of the flesh. For the flesh lusts against the spirit, and the spirit against the flesh, and these are contrary the one to the other, so that ye cannot do the things that you would. But if ye be led by the spirit ye are not under the law." Let us stop a minute and comment on this. Paul is telling us to let the spirit lead us and we will not be under the law. I remember what Jesus said in the gospels; he said; when the Holy Spirit is come he will lead you in all ways of truth and right. If we have become a new creation in Christ the Holy Spirit is living in us and wants to lead us. Now let's go on as we read the next verses take note Paul talks about the works of the flesh, and said with a strong emphasis the ones who practice such things shall not inherit the kingdom of God. Now let's read verses 19-21. "Now the works of the flesh are manifest, which are these; adultery, fornication, uncleanness, lasciviousness, idolatry, witchcraft, hatred, variance, emulations, wrath, strife, seditions, heresies, envying, murders, drunkenness, reveling, and such like; as I have told you in the past, that they who do such things shall not inherit the kingdom of God."

"Wait just a moment," said Pastor Joe. "Deacon Bill, are you trying to tell me you never do any of these things?"

"No not at all," said Deacon Bill, "I do falter sometimes, but the spirit lets me know when I fail, if I would have listened to him and do what the Bible tells us to do confess our sins to him, he would have been faithful and just to forgive me, and cleanse me from all unrighteousness, and I would have been in Heaven today."

"Let me break in," said Ann, "I believe this has turned out to be a sermon. We are out of time we will have to take this up at another time."

"Ok said," Deacon Bill, "I didn't mean to be so long on this, but I have barely touched on this subject, there is many more scriptures pertaining to the subject grace and works. One last word everyone please take your Bible and read [verses 22 thru 25] pertaining to the fruits of the spirit."

"Ok," said Ann, "I want to thank both of you for being on our program. We hope you will come back again."

Pastor Joe said "my pleasure, anytime."

"It has been great to be on your program," said Deacon Bill, "I would like to remind the audience of the seven o'clock study at the church tonight. We will be moving to the stadium tomorrow night. I would like to invite Pastor Joe to take part in our study."

"Thank you very much," said Ann, "well folks you have heard the interview with Pastor Joe and Deacon Bill. I wish we had more time in our interview, but we will have them back in the next day or so for another interview. Deacon Bill has reminded you of his study tonight at the church. We will be there live with our cameras, so tune in tonight. We must leave you now and go to our regular programming, thanks for watching."

Josie asked Stan what he thought about the interview. Stan said, "I think Deacon Bill was right on. I just wish Pastor Joe could understand what has taken place. Do you think Satan has blinded his mind to the true gospel? It seems like I have read somewhere in the Bible of Satan blinding peoples mind, so they will not believe the truth."

"I sure hope not," said Josie, "we have known our Pastor for a long time, and he is one of our best friends."

Stan and Josie turn the TV. off and begin to discuss what they are going to do during the day.

"I have an idea," said Josie, "why don't we go volunteer at the hospital or a convalescent home today, I am sure they need some help."

"That is a great idea," said Stan, "why didn't I think of that. You are a great woman. I do want to be free at one o'clock today to meet with Deacon Bill at the Agape Church and see if I can help out in the evening service as a counselor or usher."

"Sounds great," said Josie, "we can go together."

"I think we should let the boss down at the casino know we are not coming in," said Stan, "and I think I am going to tell him that I am quitting, and tell him the reason why!"

"Me too," said Josie, "I have served my last alcoholic drink to anyone. I am tired of those people blowing smoke in my face, and using bad language. Here is one other thing I am going to do if you don't mind. I am going to pour out all the liquor and beer we have in the refrigerator."

"Great," said Stan, "I will help you; from now on we are living for Jesus!"

Stan and Josie call their boss at work and tell him they are quitting. He laughs at them and calls them a couple of Jesus freaks. After talking to their boss Josie calls the hospital to see if they can volunteer. "Sure," said the administrator, "come on down we need you guys bad."

Stan and Josie head for the hospital.

Chapter 11

SIGNS OF HIS COMING

When Stan and Josie arrive at the hospital the administrator asks them what they could do best and if they have any hospital experience at all. They tell him they don't have any experience at a hospital. But Josie said, "I spent some time around the hospital when we had our children, but not much experience, but I am willing to help in any way I can."

The administrator said, "We are short on nurses and nurses' aides, maybe you can be a nurse's aide."

"Sure," said Josie, "I am willing to try."

"Ok," said the administrator, "report to the head nurse and she will get you started out." "Ok," said Josie, "I am going to wait to see what Stan is going to be doing."

Stan said, "I have an idea, I know how to clean rooms, I could also help patients get in and out of bed, I could change beds and do laundry."

"Sounds great," said the administrator, "I will send you down to housekeeping."

Stan and Josie head for their departments after telling the administrator they will have to be off for about an hour at noon, and get off at no later than 5 o'clock.

Stan and Josie meet in the cafeteria at noon and have lunch. Josie said, "How is it going."

"Great," said Stan, "I have been down in the laundry room doing laundry. I never saw so much dirty laundry in all my life, and when I say dirty that is an understatement for some of it. Some of it has quite an odor. I think they were about out of clean laundry, I suppose I will be there the rest of the day. How has it been going with you?"

"I have been changing some of the beds where your laundry has been coming from. Help has been so short they have only been changing the beds that really need it, and believe me some of them really need it. The nurses and aides are really tired they have been working almost around the clock. They run home take a shower, sleep awhile and return to the hospital. I have also been taking patient's temperature, blood pressure, help some of them with their baths, change their gowns, and give them their medicine. I have been a very busy camper."

As soon as they finish their lunch they run down to the Agape church to meet with Deacon Bill for a few minutes. Then they return to work.

At five o'clock they leave the hospital run by a fast food, get some food to take home and return home. They eat, take a shower, take a short nap, and give the Mcelliots a quick call to see if they are ready to go. They say sure we will meet you outside your garage. Stan backs the car out, Josie and the Mcelliots get in and they head for the church. They talk about the things they had been doing that day. The Mcelliots had returned to their regular jobs also.

When they arrive at the church the parking lot is almost full, and there is already a line at the door of the church waiting for the doors to open. The TV station is setting up their cameras inside.

Pastor R.B. McCartney

    Soon the parking lot is full, and a traffic jam has occurred outside the church. The police arrive and set up a barricade to keep people out of the parking lot. Cars are now parking on the streets around the church.

    Stan said, "I have an idea! I am going to talk to the police, see if they will ask the people to park at the shopping center a few blocks away. They could unload their passengers here at the church and park at the shopping center. If some of the other folks here will help me, we will shuttle them back to the church." Some of the other guys say sure we will help. Stan talks to the police, they say they think it is a great idea and they will cooperate. Stan and some of the others leave for the shopping center and begin shuttling people back to the church.

    One of the guys who Stan was shuttling to the church told Stan what had happened to his family.

    He said, "We used to attend church regular. We were very successful in life. We had a nice home, a camper, a boat, and other toys. We began to miss church on Sunday to go out to the lake, fish, water-ski, ride our dirt bikes, and picnic. We begin to make friends with other who liked to have a few beers, and we began to drink with them to be sociable. We began to miss church more and more until we finally didn't have much time for church. Either we were gone camping or we were getting everything ready to go the next weekend. We allowed our oldest son to drink beer with us; he soon became a heavy drinker, and begins to take drugs. He didn't just drink and drug on the weekend he did it all week. He was failing in school and finally got kicked out. We have had to bail him out of jail a few times, and he is now on probation. We had two younger children, which have gone in the rapture. We tried to get our older son to come along to church with us tonight, but he just made fun of us. I blame myself for what has happened to him. I think if we had remained in church and didn't begin to do the things of the world he would still be going to church and his life wouldn't be in such turmoil. The wife and I have made up our mind to get back to serving God. Please pray for us, and also pray for our son."

They arrive at the church Stan lets him out and assures him he will give him a ride back to the shopping center after the service.

Stan finishes his shuttles and goes in the church. The church is filled to capacity and many people are on the lawn, and in the parking lot outside. He finds Josie and takes his seat.

Josie said, "How did it go"

"Great," said Stan, "I am excited about the big crowd here tonight. The church is full and people are everywhere outside. I already feel blessed."

Deacon Bill opens up the service with prayer, and then said, "I have some announcements to make before we start our study. The Mayor has asked us if we will have our study tomorrow night at the stadium. He said the large crowds at our church are causing a traffic problem. We have agreed to meet there tomorrow night. If we meet there we will need the following workers. Parking Lot attendants, ushers, counselors, pianist, and song director. We are inviting pastors, and workers from other churches to help us. I have heard there are other pastors with us tonight. If you are here please meet me down front after the service. We will begin our study at this time. We are continuing our study on "Signs of his coming."

Sign #4: political unrest.

Turn to [Matthew 24:6, 7] "for nation shall rise against nation and kingdom against kingdom; and there shall be famines, pestilence, and earthquakes in divers places. We will deal with wars and rumors of war in this section: In the 20th century we have had two world wars and over 100 wars around the globe since world war two. Today many nations are developing weapons of mass destruction. It is just a matter of time until some ungodly leader will rise up and launch a nuclear war that will perhaps be greater and more destructive than all the other wars put together.

Jesus said, "As it was in the days of Noah so shall it be when he would return to the earth." This is talking about when he returns as King of Kings and Lord of Lords taking vengeance on those who are destroying the earth. We read about the times of Noah in Genesis Chapter 6 thru Chapter 8 and Luke the 17th Chapter. In Luke he talked about a time of prosperity, and a population explosion. In Genesis he mentions mans heart being continually evil and violence through out the world.

On September 11, 2001 we witnessed the worst violence the united states has ever witnessed, four planes being hijacked at one time by very violent men. The purpose was to destroy as many people as possible and to cripple the government of the USA. The first shocking news we heard was a plane had crashed into one of the towers of the World Trade Center, then not long after we heard another plane had crashed into the other tower. It was a time of shock for all of us when the TV stations began to show all the destruction of the buildings burning and collapsing with hundreds of people trapped in the buildings. We knew it was bad and many would lose their lives. Then we heard another plane had crashed into the pentagon with much destruction. Then news came of another plane crashing in a field in Pennsylvania. This plane was destined to crash into the capitol or white house, but some brave passengers and plane crew fought with the hijackers to prevent the plane from reaching the destination. It crashed in a field killing everyone aboard. These brave men and women gave their lives that others might live. Also many rescue workers died in the twin towers saving lives of other.

Since that time America has been in two major wars trying to slow down the acts of terrorism. I am sure much has been accomplished, but the threat of terrorism still remains throughout the world. When men and women are taught they are doing God's will by killing others it is evil times. In some countries even young children are being trained to strap bombs on them and blow up others. The apostle Paul said, "In the last days perilous times will come." I believe we are living in the last days.

Homeland security has been doing a good job in securing our airlines, but it is probably only a matter of time until there is a security leak allowing a lot of damage to be done either to a plane or a terminal.

What about our trains and buses? A spokesman said the other day it is almost impossible to guard all terminals and the thousands of miles of track. There was a bomb exploded on a train in another country the other day killing two hundred people and wounding others. There are possibilities of bombs being loaded on trucks being crashed into bridges or being crashed into large buildings in some of the large cities. We also have cruise ships carrying as many as two thousand people. A small boat loaded with a bomb could be launched at many unguarded boat launches, and could be crashed into a cruise ship killing many people. Yes, our security people have plenty to do in this wicked time.

Sign #5 Social Promiscuity

Turn your Bible to [II Timothy 3:3, 4.] "without natural affection, trucebreakers, false accusers, incontinent, fierce, despisers of those that are good, traitors heady, high-minded, lovers of pleasure more than lovers of God." Paul said these things are the marks of the last days. Let's look at without natural affections. We believe this is referring to the homosexual lifestyle. This defies the laws of nature. When God created mankind he created them male and female. He gave them the desire of sex that they might make love and have children to populate the earth. God also made the animals male and female to procreate the earth. The Bible also teaches sex is only to be between a man and a woman who are married.

Now let us go into the gospel of Luke and see what Jesus said about the homosexual lifestyle. [Luke 17:28-32] "likewise as it was in the days of Lot; they did eat, they drank, they bought, they sold, they planted, they builder; but the same day Lot went out of Sodom it rained fire and brimstone from heaven and destroyed them all, even thus shall it be in the day the son of man shall be revealed." Suppose we should go into the Old Testament and see how it was in the days of Lot. We read the story in genesis the 19th Chapter. Two angels go down to Sodom to destroy the city. God had said their sins were very grievous in his sight. The angels [in the form of men] enter the city and entered into Lots house to spend the night. Before they lay down to rest for the night the men of the city both young and old compass the house and begins to yell for Lot to bring the men out to them so they can have sex with them. Lot goes outside and pleads with them to not do such a wicked thing. They say they will deal with Lot and begin trying to break down the door. The angels reach and pull Lot into the house and caused the men to be blind so they couldn't see to break down the door. The angels tell Lot to get his family together and bring them out of the city because the Lord had seen the sins in the city and had sent them to destroy it. When Lot had entered the city he had many servants, besides his daughters. When Lot tells them the Lord has sent the angels to destroy the city and has said for them to get out he appears to his sons-in- laws as one who mocks. When Lot lingers the angels take hold of his hand, his wife's hand, and his daughter's hands and lead them out and tells them to escape to the mountains for safety. Lot want's to go to city of Zoar, the angels agree. Then we read when Lot entered into Zoar it rained fire and brimstone upon Sodom and Gomorrah and destroyed everyone and everything. Only Lot and his two daughters were spared. Lots wife had turned back and was destroyed. Remember this was the way Jesus said it would be when he returns.

Homosexuality is an abomination to God. The definition of abomination is something God hates greatly. This is one of the sins under the law that was punishment by death. Turn to [Leviticus 20:13] and see what the law had to say, "If a man lie with mankind as he lieth with a woman, both of them have committed an abomination; they shall surely be put to death." You may say this scripture is in the Old Testament under the law.

Ok turn in the new testament to [Romans 1: 24-28] "Wherefore God also gave them up to uncleanness thru the lust of their own hearts, to dishonor their own bodies between themselves; who changed the truth of God into a lie, and worshiped and served the creature more than the creator, who is blessed forever, amen. For this cause God gave them up to vile affections; for even the women did change the natural use into that which is against nature; likewise also the men leaving the natural use of the woman, burned in their lust one toward the other; men with men working that which is unseemly, and received in themselves that recompense of their error which was meet. And even as they did not like to retain God in their knowledge, God gave them over to a reprobate mind, to do those things which are not convenient. In the next three verses Paul mentions a lot of sins, one of them is unnatural affections, we will skip down to verse [32] and read, "who knowing the judgment of God, that they which commit such things are worthy of death, not only do the same, but have pleasure in them that do them."

I know there is going to be those who will say Deacon Bill is a gay basher. No, Deacon Bill did not say these words that have been printed, but God has said them. Now someone is going to say Deacon Bill don't you know they were born that way, and I am going to say no they weren't born that way. When babies are first born they are pure and innocent, but they are born into a sinful world with the devil and demons in it. As they grow up their brain begins to be programmed. These evil spirits begin to influence their minds to do sinful things. This is why the Bible said, [Romans 3:23] all have sinned and come short of the glory of God." We all have been sinners, some have committed one sin and other have committed other sins. But the fact is we all need Jesus.

Can a sodomite be saved? The answer is, yes they can. God loves them the same as he does the liar, the thief, the gambler, the person on drugs, the alcoholic, the fornicator, the adulterer, the busybody, and all other sins. Jesus died on the cross for everyone. He is the way the truth and the life no one can come to the father but by him. Here is what everyone has to do; hear the word, realize they are a sinner, repent of their sin, receive Jesus into their heart, and then the Holy Spirit will help us be a new person in Christ. That word Repent means to hate the sinful life we are living. If we take pride in living a sinful life we will continue to live a sinful life and will not come to the place of repentance.

Now let us look at another word incontinent. Webster describes the definition as, "without self restraint, especially in regard to sexual activity." This is not applying to just homosexuals, but to heterosexuals also. The Bible strictly teaches against fornication, and adultery, yet many who profess to be Christians practice it today. We would like to deal with these words separately.

We will deal with fornication first. Webster describes the word fornication as, "voluntary sexual intercourse between unmarried persons." We are living in a society today of loose morals. Many men and women are living together today, sleeping together committing fornication night after night. Some of them go to church every Sunday and act if there is nothing wrong with what they are doing. Then there are those who do not live together, but are having sexual relations with others during the week, and on week ends.

A lot of youth today are saying forget about dating. They talk about hooking up with friends for no strings attached sex. Have you heard of sex bracelets? These are color coded wrist bands girls wear which boys snap off their wrist. Depending on the color a boy rips off he is rewarded a sex favor. Some shows on MTV glorify random encounters of sexual aggressive young women. According to recent study done by the Rand Corporation and the University of California found that children age 12 to 17, who watched a lot of racy TV were twice as likely to have sex as those who didn't. I have just heard that a lot of teens who have taken the pledge to practice abstinence until married are having all kinds of perverted sex and just because it is not normal sex they do not think they have broken their pledge of staying abstinent until married. This doesn't stop when they graduate from high school but continues until they get married. Many of these youth do not even think about sexual transmitted disease.

Some of these people young and older go to church on Sunday thinking everything is ok between them and God.

Many programs on regular TV, are glorifying people of adult age who are unmarried, going to bed together having babies and act like it is the normal thing to do.

Some people who are committing fornication are sitting in the church pews on Sunday morning, having their conscience seared over so they don't think what they have been doing is a sin. You can mention Jesus could come any moment, and they get excited, yell praise the Lord, amen, and act if they are ready to go out to meet him.

We are living in a time when many pastors never talk about fornication from the pulpit. They are more interested in building a large church by sugar coating the gospel rather than preach against sin. They are afraid they will offend someone and make them quit coming. I do say we should encourage sinners to come to church, but God forbid if we do not preach repentance in our churches. God said we should warn the people to flee the wrath to come. It said if we see our brother or sister sin and we do not warn them their blood will be upon us.

Paul in writing to several churches had a lot to say about fornication. Let's look at some of those scriptures: look at [1Cor. 6:9-11] "know ye not the unrighteous shall not inherit the kingdom of God? Be not deceived: neither fornicators, nor idolaters, nor adulterers, nor effeminate, nor abusers of themselves with mankind, nor thieves, nor covetous, nor drunkards, nor revilers, nor extortionist, shall inherit the kingdom of God, and such were some of you, but ye are washed, but you are sanctified, but you are justified in the name of the Lord Jesus, and by the spirit of God." Then Paul tells us in [I Cor. 6:18] "Flee fornication, every sin that a man doeth is without the body; but he that committeth fornication sinneth against his own body." We must also read the [verse 19 and 20]. "What know ye not that your body is the temple of the Holy Ghost which is in you, which ye have of God, and ye are not your own. For ye are bought with a price; therefore glorify God in your body, and in your spirit, which are Gods." The scripture said flee fornication, for when we commit fornication we sin against our own body. When we receive Christ our body becomes the temple of the Holy Ghost. We have been bought with a price the precious blood of Jesus Christ therefore we should glorify God with our body. Now turn to [I Cor. 7:1-2] "now concerning the things whereof ye wrote unto me: It is good for a man not to touch a woman. Nevertheless, to avoid fornication, let every man have his own wife, and let ever woman have her own husband. I do not think the word can be any clearer. Sexual relation is only supposed to be between a man and a woman who are married, and should be refrained from out of wedlock. Paul spoke on the same line to at least five other churches.

Many parents today are indulging in adulterous living and they feel guilty when they speak to their children about fornication. Then many of children are living in a single parent home where the parent is more interested in drugs, alcohol, and partying than trying to raise their children. Many children are living in a home where the man and woman are living together out of wedlock. Then there are those who live together for years out of wedlock have children and don't even think about getting married, and some of them go to church.

Now we will take up adultery. I know this is a touchy subject in the day we are living in. Perhaps many of us here tonight have been guilty of committing adultery, and if you noticed, I said us, and included myself in the group, which have committed adultery. That is the reason I was left behind when Jesus came for his church. But I have repented and promised my Lord that it will not happen again.

First let's look in Webster's Dictionary for his definition of adultery. Here is Webster's definition, "voluntary sexual intercourse between a married person and another not the spouse." Jesus in his teachings goes a little farther than Webster. The Pharisees came to Jesus tempting Jesus and asked him the question. Is it lawful for a man to put away his wife for every cause? Remember they were asking him to see what he would say about the law. Divorce had become a very common thing with the people under the law. A man could divorce his wife over petty things like if she burned the bread, this was grounds for divorce.

Here is what Jesus said to them, [Matthew 19:4-6]"have ye not read, that he which made them at the beginning made them male and female, and said for this cause shall a man leave father and mother and shall cleave to his wife: and they twain shall be one flesh. Wherefore they are no more twain, but one flesh. What God has joined together let no man put asunder." Then the Pharisees say to him, "Why did Moses then command to give a writing of divorcement, and to put her away. Jesus said, [Matthew 19:8, 9] "Moses because of the hardness of your hearts suffered you to put away your wives: but from the beginning it was not so. And I say unto you, whosoever shall put away his wife, except it be for fornication, and shall marry another, committeth adultery: and whoso marrieth her who is put away doth commit adultery." We see how Jesus has gone farther than Webster, and said if a man divorces his wife for any cause except fornication he commits adultery.

This scripture has made divorce something that displeases God. Now before you go running out the door and turn me off please hear me out on this subject. I realize a big percentage of people who are under sixty years of age have gone through divorce, and a few older. One thing we must realize, God hates divorce, but he forgives people who have gone through divorce. There is only one unpardonable sin, and that is blaspheming the Holy Spirit. Usually Christian couples in their marriage ceremonies make a pledge before God and witnesses, until death do us part. Usually the minister performing the ceremony will tell them they shouldn't enter into marriage without serious aforethought and not without counseling. A wise counselor will tell the couple if either is not a Christian, or if they are of different faiths, it will in most cases create a problem in their marriage if they do not settle this issue before marriage. Some couples will say, "We love each other so much this would never be a problem with us." Then some of those who are a Christian will think, I will win my mate over after we are married. Sometimes this happens, but in a lot of cases it does not happen, and after much heartache the marriage comes to an end. Many times today children are involved, and they have to go through hell on earth. In the case, where someone marries a person of another faith. I have seen this to cause all kinds of problems, and sometimes results either in divorce or one of them not even going to church.

Now let's deal with divorce. Some people believe if a person goes through divorce they should remains single, and not remarry until the mate passes on. This is good if they can refrain from sex. This might work for older people but normally does not for younger people. The apostle Paul said it was better to stay single, but it was better to marry than to burn. The bottom line is God hates divorce, but he will forgive those who have gone through a divorce. Sometimes married people have to go through hell on earth trying to keep their marriage together. This could have been avoided if they would have accepted wise counsel before marriage.

Now let's look at the things, which could happen in, marriage that God said is grounds for a divorce. We read earlier where Jesus said; whosoever put away his wife, except for fornication committeth adultery. According to this scripture if either mates has another lover it is grounds for divorce. But this doesn't mean they have to get a divorce. If the mate, who is having the affair, will repent to God, break off the relationship, asks the other mate to forgive them and go straight, the marriage can be salvaged. There have been many couples where the offending one repents and asks the other mate to forgive and promises it will not happen again. The mate who has been offended forgives them and they have a happy marriage from that point till death parts them. There is one other thing that should take place. Once you have forgiven your mate, don't bring up the matter again, let it be as if it has been forgotten

I say to you if you have caught your mate sinning against you don't make divorce the first option. Make prayer the first option, and begin to pray for the offending mate, act like a Christian in all the things you do around your mate, give prayer time to work. You may win your mate, and have a happy marriage.

Now lets see what God has said about putting away mates that were none believers. In the book of Ezra the ninth and tenth Chapter, Ezra addresses the subject of marrying heathen women. He talks about how they have been enticed by women to serve other Gods; King Solomon was one of the kings who let heathen wives cause him to worship idols. God tells them through Ezra to put away their heathen wives, and they make a covenant with God to put them away according to the law. What had happened here, they had married into races that were not Jewish which served other Gods, and not the Lord God. They worshiped idol Gods, and influenced their mate to worship them also. This was strictly forbidden by the Lord God of Israel.

Paul gives instruction to Christians on being married to an unbeliever in [I Corinthians 7:12-16] let's read what he said, "but to the rest speak I, not the Lord: If any brother has a wife that believeth not, and she is pleased to dwell with him let him, not put her away. And the woman that hath a husband that believeth not, and if he be pleased to dwell with her, let her not leave him. For the unbelieving husband is sanctified by the wife and the unbelieving wife is sanctified by the husband: else were your children unclean; but now are they holy, but if the unbelieving depart. A brother or sister is not under bondage in such cases: but God has called us to peace, for what knowest thou, o wife, whether thou shall save thy husband? Or how knowest thou, o man, whether thou shall save your wife." Paul is saying if the unbelieving mate will allow the Christian mate to go to church, serve God and bring the children up in church without complaining, and he or she is a good mate there is no grounds to depart, but if the mate is not willing to do this let the mate depart. The bottom line is the wife or husband may be able to lead the other mate to the Lord. There have been those that lived with a non-Christian for years, which was a good person. Some of them would help work around the church and never did accept Christ. But there are those after many years of being a non-believer have accepted Christ. There is a saying, where there is life there is hope.

The bottom line is, we are living in the last days. It is no wonder Paul spoke about the latter times to Timothy as he did, lets read what he said, [I Timothy 4:1-3] " now the spirit speaketh expressly, that in the latter times some shall depart from the faith, giving heed to seducing spirits, and doctrines of devils; speaking lies in hypocrisy; having their conscience seared with a hot iron; I believe the things we have spoken about tonight indicates we are living in the last days, and those who are living in sin need to take inventory of their life and repent before it is too late.

Now let's talk about the sixth sign of his coming.

Sign #6: Natural Disaster:

When Jesus' disciples asked him in the twenty fourth Chapter of Matthew what would be the signs of his coming he said one of the signs would be earthquakes in diver's places. In my life time I have seen earthquakes more frequent every year that passes by and more intensified. Earthquakes have been happening all over the world with many thousand people being killed. I am sure everyone here tonight can remember the one which has recent happened causing the tsunamis in south Asia killing over 200,000 people and Billions of dollars in damage. Now there has been a really bad quake in Pakistan which has already been responsible for over 80,000 deaths. Then of course there have been those in Japan, turkey, Iran, and other countries overseas.

Many of the states in the U.S.A. have been having earthquakes, but to date California has been hit harder than any other state. In the past forty years there have been too many quakes in California to count. There have been three disastrous quakes in metropolitan areas with many killed, and Billions of dollars in damage. These were quakes where freeway bridges collapsed trapping many people under twisted steel and concrete. Many homes, hospital, and commercial buildings were destroyed. Now they say the big one is yet to come. Jesus said in the book of revelation. An earthquake would happen in the last days where the islands would move out of their place, and the mountains would disappear. So I guess we haven't seen anything yet.

While California has had her part of earthquakes there has also been many fires and floods, and not only in California but throughout the USA. The east coast has been having disastrous hurricanes with loss of life and property. The year 2005 was the worse year for hurricanes ever recorded. We had hurricane Katrina which devastated the gulf coast destroying homes and businesses in Alabama, Mississippi, and Louisiana. Many complete cities were completely destroyed with many deaths. The levies in New Orleans were broken causing flooding to many homes. Many people had to get on their roofs to be rescued from the water. Also the high waves created by the hurricane surged over many homes along the coast causing much destruction and loss of lives and property. Check this scripture out in [Luke 21:25] "And there will be signs in the moon, and in the stars; and on the earth distress of nations with perplexity, the sea and waves roaring." Our President said Katrina was the worse natural disaster ever to happen in the United States. Then just a few days later here comes Rita causing much damage along the Texas coast, then hurricane Wilma hits Florida and causes much damage there. A Lot of people are still homeless from these hurricanes, and will be for months to come. Yes I think we have been living in the signs of his coming.

I have been saying all of these things to try and convince everyone that these signs have taken place, Jesus has come in the rapture for his church and you and I have been left behind. But I want you to know tonight you can still go to be with your family if you will repent of your sins, and live for Jesus from here on. It is not going to be easy because we will have to refuse the mark of the beast, and not be able to buy or sell. We will literally starve to death if we are not killed before we starve.

If you haven't repented of your sins in these meetings, or if you haven't received Jesus as your Lord and savior we are going to invite you to do so tonight. I am going to have you to make the most important decision you have ever made.

Pastor R.B. McCartney

If you are here and feel your heart is not right with God I am going to ask you to raise your hand. Get your hand up high. Yes, yes, I see those hands. Now I am going to ask you to stand to your feet and repeat a simple prayer after me. You who are outside watching the monitors can also do the same. Now repeat this prayer after me. Dear Lord, I realize I have been unfaithful to your word. --------I repent of my sins. ----------- I promise to live for you from here on. -------- Please forgive me, and cleanse my heart. ---------in Jesus name I pray

If you have said this prayer from your heart Jesus has forgiven you and cleansed you from all unrighteousness. Before you leave will you please come down front, and we will give you some literature to help you grow.

At this time we will ask everyone to stand for prayer?" Deacon Bill prays a prayer of thanksgiving for the good service which has taken place everyone shakes hands, hugs each other and begins to leave

Josie and the Mcelliots visit with other people at the church while Stan shuttles people back to the shopping center. After everyone has been delivered to the shopping center, Stan finds Josie and the Mcelliots and they head for home.

On the way home they talk about some of the things Deacon Bill has been teaching. Stan said, "Deacon Bill talked about things tonight I have never heard our Pastor Joe say much about. In fact he never did say anything about homosexuality being a sin, and I have never heard him say anything about fornication. In fact I believe we had at least two couples who were living together and weren't married, and they had positions in the church. I believe one of the ladies was teaching kids in Sunday school."

"Yes," said Josie, "I had never thought anything about it until tonight. One of those couples had three children and had been living together for several years. I just thought if they were living together and was raising a family it was ok. My ears and eyes were opened tonight when Deacon Bill gave the definition of fornication. I had never thought too much about it being a sin when people were living together and not being married. I just thought when they lived together and raised children it was the same as being married. I don't think I had ever heard the word fornication until tonight."

"Yes," said Mr. Mcelliots, "I had never given it much thought. I wasn't going to church and I didn't hear much about the things Deacon Bill was addressing tonight. Of course I was as big a hypocrite as them."

"Yes," said Mrs. Mcelliot, "you sure were. I use to say we need to get in church and you would say, I am just as good as those church people, and you were good to me and the children. But you weren't helping us to learn about the Lord. We both were neglectful about learning God's word. That is the reason we were left behind when Jesus came for our children."

They arrive home; the Mcelliots say good night and go to their home. Stan and Josie go into the house turn on the TV for a few minutes to see what is going on around the world. Then turn in for the night.

Chapter 12

WHY WE WERE LEFT BEHIND.

Stan and Josie had spent their day working at the hospital. Although they had gone to Agape Church at 1:00 pm to sign up to be counselors for the night service at the stadium. Deacon Bill instructed the counselors to come down front during the altar call. He also instructed them on what they were to do. After they received instructions on what to do Stan and Josie returned to the hospital to work.

They worked until about 5:00 o'clock and headed for home. "Let's stop and get fast food tonight," said Josie.

"Good enough for me," said Stan, "that way we will not be late for service tonight."

When they arrive at home they talk with the Mcelliots. The Mcelliots have signed up to be ushers at the stadium. They tell Stan and Josie they will take their car to the service because they will have to be there early to be ushers. Stan and Josie turn on the news, and crash in their chairs for a few minutes rest.

The biggest news is talking about Bar-Jesus and how he is going to have the answers to where everyone is gone, and how he is going to bring peace to the world. Details are still being worked out to make him the leader of the world.

Stan and Josie get cleaned up, and head for the stadium. When they get there the stadium is already beginning to fill up. Praise God, said Josie; "I am excited about tonight. I never knew church could be so much fun."

"Me neither," said Stan; it makes me feel good to know we are doing something for Jesus, but I know we will never be able to do as much for him as he has for us."

At seven o'clock the stadium is almost full. Deacon Bill comes to the podium. You can tell he is filled with joy by the expression on his face because. He said; "praise God, isn't it wonderful to see so many people out on a Friday night, and it is wonderful to see everyone can be inside tonight for the service. We appreciate the Mayor making the arrangements so we could use the stadium tonight. Thank you very much Mr. Mayor. I believe our Mayor is here tonight. Mr. Mayor, will you please stand. There he is in the middle section please give him a good hand of applause. Tonight we are honored to have Brother Robert, music minister from one of our Baptist Churches. We will let Brother Robert tell you why he was left behind before he leads us in music. We are also glad to have Sister Phyllis from the Methodist church to play the piano for us. At this time we would like to have Sis Phyllis come to the piano, and Bro. Robert come to direct our singing. We would like for Bro. Robert to give his testimony before he begins the music."

Bro. Robert comes to the podium and greets everyone, and then he begins to give his testimony. "I was saved many years ago; I had majored in music in college. Not long after I was saved I was elected as minister of music in the church we were attending; I was also a respected business man in town. My company had contracts with the government, and we were doing ok in business and making a living. Then I discovered if you lie and cheat the government, pay off a few people here and there we could make more money. Making more money we were, but making more money didn't seem to make us any happier. In fact I seemed to always have guilt about the way I was conducting our business. I did read the Bible. And I knew it taught against lying, stealing, and cheating. I kept telling myself I was going to start being honest, but Satan would say to me, "everyone is stealing a little from the government, it is ok as long as everyone else is doing it," so that would soothe my conscience for that moment. When we woke up this week and our loved ones were missing, I knew I had been left behind. I had heard our Pastor say a few days back, "Jesus was going to be coming for the church soon, and he was encouraging everyone to be ready. This has really taught me a lesson. I would give all the money I have if I could change things, and be with my family but it is too late for that, but thank God it isn't too late to go be with them again soon. I am going to start serving Jesus today. I am determined from now on I will be faithful to the Bible, and the Lord. I know there is going to be some trying times just ahead, but from here out I will be faithful unto death. Ok that is enough of my testimony, I am sure a lot of you have a similar testimony. Turn in your hymnals to page 297 "what a friend we have in Jesus." Now let's hear you sing it like you mean it." Everyone was singing, and what a great sound coming from the stadium. Next they "sung the old rugged cross," "amazing grace," "how great thou art," and last "when we all get to heaven." You could tell everyone was really enjoying the singing, because everyone in the stadium was singing.

 Josie whispers to Stan, "now that is what I call singing." Stan nods his head yes.

 Deacon Bill comes back to the podium and said, "wasn't that good singing, you guys really sound good, and now lets give our pianist and song director a good hand of applause," the applause could be heard several blocks away. "Now let's hear Sister Phyllis' testimony."

Phyllis comes to the podium and greets everyone. She said, "I guess you all wonder why I didn't go in the rapture. I was probably in the same boat with some of you. I had hidden sin in my life. I was living one way around the church members, and another way around others. I talked about the church members behind their back. I talked about my neighbors, and everyone I came in contact with. I guess I was what they call a busy body. Instead of praying for them I was always condemning them and judging them, when at the same time I was committing the same sins they were. I couldn't wait to hear a rumor, so I could tell it to others. I knew this was wrong, and I needed to repent, but every time I would think of repenting Satan would tell me I was as good as everyone else. I would listen to him instead of the Holy Spirit. My husband and children have gone in the rapture. I miss them very much, and wish I could be with them. Through Deacon Bills study I have come to realize why I have been left behind. I have repented of the things I was doing and, I have a new life now, and I am looking forward to seeing my family again in heaven. From now on I plan on seeking after the things of the spirit, instead of the things of the flesh. Instead of talking about everyone, I will be praying with them and for them. God bless everyone and don't forget to pray for me."

"Thank you sister Phyllis," said Deacon Bill as he comes back to the podium "I am sure some of you tonight have been riding in the same boat as Sister Phyllis, and myself, or you wouldn't be here tonight. After we have a word of prayer we want to address the subject, **"why we have been left behind,"** Let's pray. Father we realize everyone here tonight has been left behind, if they hadn't been left behind they would be in heaven tonight instead of here. Tonight as we bring forth your word, please lead us as we teach, in Jesus name we pray. Now let's address "why we have been left behind." I believe you will agree with me, we have all missed the mark and been left behind, Jesus has come for the bride and we have been left behind. There is one of two reasons why we have been left behind. Number one, some of you had not been born again, then number two, some of us had received Christ into our lives, but we had let sin begin to rule in our lives. We were going around with un-confessed sin's in our lives, which was grieving the Holy Spirit. The Holy Spirit tried to tell us we needed to repent because Jesus was coming soon, but because Satan and sin was ruling us and we wouldn't listen to the Holy Spirit He had been grieved and left us on our own to live a miserable life in our sins. We had let the things of the world come into our lives and had wound up in the pig pen like the Prodigal Son. Sometimes a person has to get into the pig pen and get covered with filth to realize how much better it was in the Fathers house. It is then we will confess our sins and head for home. John said this in [I John 1:9] "If we confess our sins, He [Christ] will be faithful and just to forgive us our sins and to cleanse us from all unrighteousness." When we do our part the Lord will do his part and forgive us. Just remember the Lord wants us to have a good life. If Satan has you bound with sinful habits that are making your life miserable, God still loves you and wants a better life for you. He just wants you to get up out of that filth confess you have sinned and start asking Him to help you. God is faithful to honor his word, and He can help you over come any habit.

Now lets deal with the subject "New Birth" or born again. There are many people today that do not know what we are talking about when we say "born again," and the reason for this is preachers are not teaching "new birth" today. Some years back I heard a preacher say, "He would not go into the subject of being born again." I think he was failing to teach his congregation the basic truth of the Bible... Jesus strictly said, "Ye must be born again." They are preaching love. Truly love is taught in the Bible, but God doesn't just love the Christians, He loves the whole world. Lets read [John 3:16] "for God so loved the world that he gave his only begotten son that whosoever believes in him should not perish, but have everlasting life." Notice it isn't our love, but it was through Gods love for us he made a way we could have everlasting life. Did you notice in the last part of the verse what the sinner has to do to obtain this everlasting life? It was believing on Jesus that sinners are saved, or in the context of the chapter [John Chapter 3] "born again." Notice the seventeenth verse "he that believeth on him is not condemned; but he that believeth not is condemned already." Now turn to the first epistle of John [Chapter 4:verse 10] "herein is love, not that we loved God, but that he loved us, and sent his son to be the propitiation [regain Gods will to sinners] for our sin. The Bible said, "In Adam all die, in Jesus all are made alive." In the book of genesis God had given man everything that he needed. He had placed him in a beautiful garden. God told man he could eat of all the trees of the garden but one. The tree God forbid him from eating was the "tree of knowledge of good and evil" God told Adam that if he ate of that tree, the day he would eat thereof he would surely die. I am sure you all know the story how Satan in the form of a serpent tricked eve into eating of the tree. He told her she would be like God. When she tasted it tasted good so she ate, and then gave to Adam, and he ate. The Bible says, "There is pleasure in sin for a season." But the pleasure doesn't last very long the penalty has to be paid. Adam and Eve found themselves hiding from God; their guilt was separating them from God. God would not have fellowship with them anymore, because they had disobeyed his rules. He would have to drive them out of the garden to keep them from eating of the tree of life and live for ever in sin, and being separated from God."

Although God still loved man, he hated sin and since man was a sinner he could not have fellowship with him, but God had a plan, which could bring man back into fellowship with him. God had told Adam when he eat of the tree he would die. God would require man to bring an animal sacrifice. This animal would be killed and shed his blood for mans sin. Then the animal would be placed on the altar as a sacrifice unto God. God made the first sacrifice, and used the skin to clothe Adam and Eve. We read about Cain and Abel, and how God accepted Abel's sacrifice because Abel was sacrificing an animal, which was required. Cain presented his of grain, which God refused, because it wasn't what God required. I think you know the story from there. This animal sacrifice was required until the day Jesus died upon the cross and shed his blood for our sins. The apostle Paul tells in his letter to the Hebrews about this sacrifice having to be made every year and did not make the person perfect, but would just last for a year. Lets read what he said in [Hebrews 10:1; 11,12] "for the law having a shadow of good things to come, and not the very image of things, can never by these sacrifices which they offered year by year continually make the comers perfect." Now lets read [verse 11 and 12], "and every priest standeth daily offering oftentimes the same sacrifices, which can never take away sins: but this man [Jesus] after he had offered one sacrifice for sins for ever, sat down on the right hand of God." Paul is talking about Jesus shedding his blood on "Calvary's cross" for our sins. After his sacrifice there wouldn't be any other sacrifice. Jesus said, "I am the way, the truth and the life no man can come to the father, but by me." If you are here tonight and haven't received Jesus into your life you need to invite him in tonight. He is standing at your hearts door wanting to come in. When he comes in you will receive new life, and your fellowship with God will be restored.

Here is the thing the Bible said we have to do to have new life in Christ. [Number one: **believe**]; to believe it takes faith. The Bible, said, "Faith comes by hearing and hearing by the word of God." [Number two: **repent**], repent means changing your thinking or going in a different direction. When we were sinners we were following the ways of sin, but one day, we heard the word of God and realized we were traveling down the road of death, and destruction. We realized we were following the wrong person. [Satan] it was then we saw Jesus being crucified on Calvary's cross shedding his blood for us, and saying, "come unto me all ye that are weary and heavy laden, and I will give you rest." It was then we received Jesus into our life. **[Receive],** was the third thing we needed to do. Jesus said. "Behold I stand at the door and knock, if anyone will open the door, I will come in". After we let him in we need to do the fourth thing, [**confess** Him] as our Lord and Savior. [Romans 10:9,] said, "If thou will confess with thou mouth the Lord Jesus, and shall believe in thy heart that God has raised him from the dead, thou shall be saved. For with the heart man believeth unto righteousness, and with the mouth confession is made unto salvation." Now let's repeat the four things we must do, which are, **believe, repent, receive** and, **confess.** If you will do these four things you will become a new person in Christ. [born again] the Apostle Paul said in his second letter to the Corinthian Church, "therefore if any man be in Christ, he is a new creation; old things are passed away; behold all things are become new." After this has taken place there is one more thing you should do, and that is be

baptized. Baptism has nothing to do with our salvation, but it represents to the world we have crucified our old man of sin on the cross, and we are being buried with Christ. Then we are raised into a new life in Christ. Here is what the apostle Paul said about baptism; [Romans 6:4] "therefore we are buried with him by baptism into death; that like Christ was raised from the dead by the glory of the father, even so we should also walk in newness of life." I think it would be good if we also quote verse 6, "knowing this, that our old man has been crucified with him, that the body of sin might be destroyed, that henceforth we should not serve sin." What this is saying is that the old sinful life we had been living was nailed to cross 2,000 years ago.

When we do the four things described, his blood is applied to our life, the Holy Spirit comes into our life and we become a new person, then the old sinful person we were is buried with him into baptism.

If you are in either of these categories I urge you to make things right with the Lord this night

We are planning a baptism Sunday afternoon at two o'clock. We will not have a service on Sunday morning. This will give everyone an opportunity to go to your own church. I will not be teaching anywhere Sunday morning, but will be speaking on baptism Saturday night. We will have our baptism on Sunday at 2:00 p.m. At this time we will ask Bro... Robert to come and lead us in an invitation number, if you need to be born again or rededicate your life will you please come down front, we want to pray with you."

Bro. Robert comes to the podium. Sis Phyllis comes to the piano. Sister Phyllis begins to play "Just as I am." Bro. Robert starts leading the number and asks everyone to sing. Deacon Bill moves to the altar. The counselors start forward, Deacon Bill tells those that need prayer to come forward, the ball field begins to fill with people, Deacon Bill, urges everyone to move in close. When the song is finished, and the last person has arrived on the field Deacon Bill said, "We would like for you to repeat this prayer. Jesus I realize that I am a sinner, I cannot save myself, I believe you died on the cross for my sins. I repent of my sins and am willing to turn from them, I receive you into my heart as my Lord, and Savior, I will confess to the world what you have done for me, amen. "If you said this prayer from your heart and really meant the prayer you have been saved." Now we will ask you to remain around for awhile while the counselors pray talk with you and give you some literature."

Here is a word of importance I think I should repeat. We are planning a baptism Sunday afternoon at 2:o'clock those who have received Jesus this week may follow the lord in baptism. We will not have a service on Sunday morning. This will give everyone an opportunity to go to your own church. I will not be teaching anywhere Sunday morning, but will be speaking on baptism Saturday night. We will have our baptism on Sunday at 2:00 P.M.

The counselors were greeting those that had come forward with a hug. Everyone seems to be very happy; Deacon Bill has a smile from ear to ear, and is praising God. No one seems to be in a hurry to leave. They are all praising God and having a good time. Someone was overheard saying, "I didn't know church could be this much fun." After awhile some begin to leave.

After praying with different one's Stan and Josie decide it is time to go home. Josie asks Stan, "how many do you think was at the stadium tonight."

He said, "I would say there were about seven or eight thousand in the stadium tonight."

"Praise God," said Josie, "there must have been at least a thousand who came forward, and I think this has been the happiest night of my life."

Yes said Stan, "it has really been a good evening, it is better than anything the world has to offer."

On the way out they see the Mcelliots, Maria's sister and Brother in law, and many others they knew, everyone was hugging and showing their love. As they go outside to the parking lot they see people with signs protesting the services, these are the people who have hardened their hearts to the gospel and don't believe the word of God. They are calling the Christians "liars." They are saying bad things to those leaving, but praise God, the Christians are turning the other cheek, and saying, "Jesus loves you." Stan and Josie arrive home and turn in for the night.

Chapter 13

JOHN DOLITTLE SWORN IN AS PRESIDENT

S tan and Josie get out of bed early, and turn on the news. They want to find out what is going on around the world. The local news is talking about the revival going on at the stadium, and the large number that had attended. They estimated about 8,000 in the service last night, and over 1,000 accepting Christ. The reporter said, "I never remember our town having a revival like we are having now." She was also talking about the protesters who were calling the people leaving the stadium names, and calling them all liars. She said, "one of the reporters had interviewed the one who seemed to be the leader of the protesters. He had said it was against separation of church and state for the services to be held in the stadium, and they were asking the ACLU to investigate. They said they would be back on Saturday night in force. The Mayor has said he would have them arrested if they do not protest orderly.

The city is slowly beginning to function normally. The emergency rooms are not as crowded as they were, thanks to volunteers who have been donating their time at the hospitals, and the convalescent homes. The city is reporting their maintenance crews are still behind on service calls, but things are improving. They are asking everyone to be patient.

Elsewhere in our nation, and in other nations which were Christian, there are reports of revival everywhere. We would like to take you at this time to our national news headquarters in New York."

"Good morning; this is Thomas Novak reporting from New York. On our national front things seem to be improving, but we have quite a ways to go before everything returns to normal. There is reported a shortage of workers in about every trade, but people are doing all they can to get things back to normal. There appears to be a Christian revival taking place in our nation. Cities all over are reporting great revival taking place. They are moving their meetings to auditoriums and stadiums to hold all the people attending. They are teaching that the people missing have been caught up to be with Jesus, and they are now with him in paradise.

They are convincing the people who are attending their meetings if they will repent, and turn to Jesus they will soon be going up also. While others believe these Christians are all liars, and Jesus has not come for anyone, but those who are missing are being hid out somewhere by the churches. Some think aliens from another planet have taken them away. I don't think anyone really knows for sure where everyone is gone, but we know this one thing for sure, it has left some of the world in a mess. We would like to hear from Tom Brown our Washington reporter at this time."

"Good morning, this is Tom Brown reporting from Washington DC. Although we still have several key people missing, our capitol has begun to function again. A new President has been sworn in. John Doolittle has been sworn in as our President, a new vice President will be selected soon. President Doolittle is getting ready to speak at this time; lets go to the oval office and listen to what he has to say."

"Good morning fellow Americans. Early this morning I was sworn in to be your President. Earlier this week our President, Vice President, Speaker of the house, and many of our Congress and Senate all were reported missing. Prior to today I was temporarily handling the affairs of our country in the absence of the President. Those of the house and senate who are still around have determined our President is not going to be returning, but if he does, he will take over as President again. It is believed by many that indeed the Lord Jesus Christ has returned for his church. We do know our President regardless of his mistakes was a good man, and said he was a Christian. I don't think our President would just vacate his office, and not mention it to anyone. We have been meeting with some of the well read prophecy teachers this week, which had been left behind. I have asked them the question, if Jesus has returned, why have you been left behind? They have told me the reason they have been left behind is because they were caught off guard and were living with un-confessed sins in their lives. Here is what one said to me. He said, and I quote.

"I had been preaching Bible prophecy for several years. I had even set dates when the **Lord** was coming. One of those dates was the year 2,000. Many of our prophecy preachers were doing the same thing, but the year 2,000 came, and everything didn't happen as we thought it would. Most of us knew the scripture where Jesus had said, "Of that day and hour knowest no man, not even the angels in heaven but my father only." But I had also read in Paul's writings in I Thessalonians the fifth Chapter, where after Paul had mentioned the church being caught out in the fourth Chapter he continues on the same subject in the fifth

Chapter. Here is what he said [I Thess 5:1-6] "but of the times and seasons, brethren, ye have no need that I write to you. For yourselves know perfectly that the day of the Lord so cometh as a thief in the night. For when they shall say, peace and safety; then suddenly destruction cometh upon them, as travail upon a woman with child; and they shall not escape. But ye brethren are not in darkness, that that day should overtake you as a thief. Ye are all children of light, and the children of day: we are not of the night, nor of darkness. Therefore let us not sleep, as others do, but let us watch and be sober." I had repeated these scriptures many times, and should have known better than to predict a day, but Satan influenced me to predict the day. It just seemed right with so many saying everything was going to happen when Y2K rolled around. I knew what Paul had said about the times and the seasons, and for sure we were in the very times the prophecies in the Bible had predicted.

I guess I was a little disappointed in God, because he didn't come when we had predicted. It had made me look like a fool. I had even written a book about Jesus returning when Y2K rolled around, I felt God had let me down. So what did I do, instead of taking credit for my mistake, I shook my fist in Gods face and blamed him for my mistake. I went down to a bar and begin to drink, and that is not all, I met a young lady and committed adultery with her. I should have known Satan was behind all of it, and I was playing in his back yard. I continued this life style until this past week and the Lord came for the church and I wasn't ready. As soon as I saw my wife and family gone I knew for sure what had happened, the Lord had come and I had been left behind. I fell upon my knees, and wept asking God to forgive me for blaming him, and for my backsliding. It was then God directed me to this scripture in [Matthew 24:42-51] "watch therefore: for ye know not what hour your Lord doth come. But know this, if the

Goodman of the house had known what hour the thief would come, he would have watched, and would not have suffered his house to be broken up. Therefore be ye also ready: for in such hour as ye think not the son of man cometh. Who then is a faithful and wise servant, whom his Lord has made him ruler over his household, to give them meat [the word] in due season? Blessed is that servant, whom the Lord when he cometh shall find doing. Verily I say unto you, that he shall make him ruler over all his goods. But and if that evil servant shall say in his heart, my Lord delayeth his coming; and shall begin to smite his fellow-servant, and to eat and drink with the drunken; the Lord of that servant will come in a day he looketh not for him, and in an hour that he is not aware of, and shall cut him asunder, and appoint him his portion with the hypocrites: there shall be weeping and gnashing of teeth". I had studied Matt 24 many times and knew this scripture. But Satan had set a trap for me, and I fell into Satan's hands. As I analyzed this scripture I realized I was no better than that person in church who had been pretending he was a Christian, and never had been saved. By Gods grace and the leadership of the Holy Spirit, I don't intend on making this mistake again. I made my promise to God I will live for him from now on regardless of the cost."

"Fellow Americans you have heard his testimony word per word as we recorded it. Although I have not been very religious since I grew up I was taught the Bible when I was young. I do believe the Bible to be the word of God, but I never have paid much attention to the Bible since I grew up. I have been too busy making money, and having a good time. But now I am beginning to take some serious thoughts concerning the Bible. Something is sure going on in many places of the world; a lot of people seem to be accepting Christianity. I do realize I am going to need a lot of help from someone smarter than me to make decisions that will have to be made in the next few weeks. I covet your prayers. Pray I will seek Gods help in leading this great country of ours. I will be meeting with world leaders next week to determine what direction we should take concerning Bar Jesus. He has already worked out a peace treaty. Our troops and the enemy have laid down their arms at the present time. Israel and the Arabs have traced Bar Jesus' roots, and he appears to have both Arab, and Israelite roots. His Jewish roots trace back to the tribe of Judah, and his Arab roots trace back to Ishmael. The Jews and the Arabs believe him to be the man to bring peace to their nations. We do know something is going on good in that part of the world. The hate the Arabs and Jews have toward one another seems to be diminishing since Bar Jesus has come on the scene. They are now embracing one another with love; they are telling any one which might be planning a terrorist attack to cool it. We will keep our country informed on future developments. We will now return you to Thomas Novak in New York."

"Ok you have heard from Washington DC. The news as a whole is looking much better. We hope everything works out with this new President, which has been sworn in. We also hope this Bar Jesus can bring peace to the world. As more news develops we will keep you informed. We will now return you to your local programming."

"You have just heard from New York and Washington. We would like to remind you of the services in the stadium tonight. There will be more news at noon, so have a good morning, and we will see you at noon."

Josie said to Stan, "why don't we go out for breakfast."

"Ok with me," said Stan.

After getting ready for the day Stan and Josie leave for the hospital.

They stop at a fast food restaurant and have breakfast. Everyone seems to be in a talking mood. Some are very excited about the revival going on in the city. Some of them had been in the services last night and seem to be bubbling over with joy. Stan and Josie talk with one man who said he was a cross country trucker. His name was Mike. Mike had arrived home this morning after a long trip. He talked about everything, which had happened on his trip. He said the highways had been a mess with accidents all over. Mike said, "He was driving down the highway when up ahead of him an eighteen-wheeler began to gradually go off on the shoulder of the interstate. He thought the driver had dozed off and would probably wake up when he crossed the ridges on the side, but to his surprise the truck kept going off into the field, jackknifing and then turning over. He knew it was bad so he started to stop his truck to render help. He was sure the driver would be dead or hurt very badly. When he got stopped he ran out to the truck to see what he could do. He looked in thru the windshield that was broken out. To his surprise there wasn't anyone in the truck but it looked like the drivers clothes and shoes were scattered in the cab. He said he looked all around, and other people had stopped and were looking also, but no one could find a body. Then someone said they wondered what had happened to all the traffic on the interstate. There just wasn't any traffic at all; there wasn't a car or truck, which wasn't stopped. Mike said, he called 911 but wasn't able to get through for awhile. When he finally got through to the dispatcher he said everything was a mess, there were reports of accident everywhere with people being injured and killed and then some of the people were missing. One man said his wife and children had just disappeared out of the car leaving their clothes behind. The dispatcher said, "I have never seen anything like this since I have been on the force. We have officers on duty that we have not been able to reach on the radio. We have called in replacements but can't reach some of them; others have said they couldn't come in until they find their family members.

We are swamped with calls, give us your location and we will send someone out as soon as possible, but don't expect it to be soon." Mike said, he waited a couple of hours there, but when no help showed up and there was no sign of life he climbed in his truck and got on the road but didn't go far until he began to see other wrecks with some missing and others badly injured. It seemed everyone was in shock, and did not know what to do, or what had happened. I spent most of the day helping the injured and waiting for the police and the paramedics.

Mike said he finally arrived at a truck stop about dark. He was exhausted all he wanted to do was get a little food and rest for the night. It looked like everyone had the same idea the place was packed and they were short of help. Some of the waitresses and cooks were missing; some had gone home to try to find their loved ones. Those that were still there had been working all day and some of the night shift hadn't showed up. When Mike entered the restaurant he was told the waitresses were all back in the kitchen and everyone would have to wait upon themselves. No one was jolly, but everyone was very solemn, and everyone was wondering what had taken place. Then someone mentioned the rapture of the church. Mike said when he heard this he thought he would call his family and see what was going on at home. When he finally got through there was no answer only his answering machine came on. He called one of his friends and received the word his family was reported missing.

Mike said he knew then what had happened, the rapture had taken place and he had been left behind. He said, "I got down on my knees in the middle of the restaurant and asked God to forgive me of my sins." He said he had gone to church with his family when he was home, but didn't live the Christian life out on the road. When Mike finally got his food he crawled into his truck and rested for the night. The next morning, after he had some coffee and some food he got back on the road, and headed for his destination. He said the interstate looked like a battle field with abandoned cars and trucks everywhere. Tow trucks and paramedics were still on the job still moving vehicles, and picking up the injured. He said as he continued to his destination the service in most restaurants was lousy. Some of them had cooks missing, some had waitresses missing. In some restaurants the cooks were serving the food to the customers, and some of the restaurants the waitresses were doing the cooking. He said some places you almost had to cook your own food. He said most of the people who were still around said those missing were good Christians, and had witnessed to them about Jesus, and that he was going to return for the Christian at any moment. Mike said the warehouse where he was to unload was backed up with trucks because of shortage of help and it had taken him two days to get unloaded. As soon as he got unloaded he headed home non-stop empty.

He had just gotten in and was having breakfast at the fast food restaurant before going home to rest. We told him about the service at the stadium at 7:00 p.m. and wished him good luck and headed for the hospital.

When Stan and Josie arrive at the hospital they went to work. Stan was going around to some of the rooms collecting and leaving laundry. He had prayed with several patients, and some of them had received Jesus into their heart. Josie had also been praying with some of the patients.

When they met for lunch they both had stories to tell of people getting saved. Josie said, "I was talking to this one woman when her husband came in. She had told me they had gone to church earlier in life but had dropped out after being hurt by the pastor her husband had been in the hospital having surgery. He was real sick and the pastor or deacons didn't even call to see about him. She said they probably could have gone to another church, but Satan used that to get them out of church. They had said they could serve God as good at home as they could in church, but they soon forgot about serving the Lord. I prayed with them and they both accepted Christ. Praise God!

Stan said, "I met a man who was eighty years old. I told him about the love of Jesus, and how he had died for our sins. He said he believed in Jesus but never had received him into his heart. I prayed the sinner's prayer with him. He received Jesus into his heart and became a brother in Christ. I am still rejoicing," As soon as they finished lunch they went back to work.

They worked until 4 o'clock and then headed for home so they could rest some before going to the night service. They both had a lot of testimonies to tell on the way home. When they arrived home they both took a nap before getting ready for the evening service.

Chapter 14

BELIEVERS BAPTISM

Stan and Josie leave home a little early so as to arrive at the stadium early. They wanted to arrive a little early for a counselors' meeting. When they arrive at the stadium Deacon Bill is meeting with several church leaders, some of them pastors and some of them associate pastors which were left behind in the rapture. They had repented of their sins after the rapture had taken place, and now were living for Christ. They were going to be helping Deacon Bill on Sunday in the mass baptism service. Deacon Bill had asked one of the pastors to be in charge of the counselors.

The Pastor's name was David. Pastor David took us aside at the stadium and instructed us on what to do when the altar call would be given. He gave us some literature on what takes place when we get saved, baptism, and Christian growth. We were instructed when the invitation song would begin we would start down to the platform on the field. Kneeling benches had been erected around the platform for people to kneel and pray. This was a little strange to some of us; we had never been used to kneeling to pray. We had always prayed sitting or standing. But no one complained at all. How could we complain when the spirit of the Lord was so strong in the services? Pastor David pointed out that in the Bible most of those who prayed were on their knees or fell on their face before God. He instructed us, when everyone had arrived at the altars Deacon Bill would have a prayer with them, and then we counselors would take them one on one, pray with them, get their name and phone number, give them literature on being saved, baptism, and Christian growth. We should also encourage them to be baptized.

Soon the stadium was packed. There were only a few seats left in the bleachers. Deacon Bill comes to the platform. He lets out a big "praise the Lord, do you love Jesus." People said amen all over the stadium. The Holy Spirit was present in a marvelous way. Deacon Bill welcome's everyone to the service, and then turns the song service over to Bro Robert.

Bro. Robert comes to the podium has a word of prayer and then ask the people if they are ready to worship God. Everyone yells out a big amen, some yelled praise the Lord hallelujah. Bro Robert said, "I can tell the spirit is here with us tonight." Sis Phyllis comes to the piano and the singing begins. The first song was "sweet Holy Spirit." Then "we sang power in the blood." The next song was "O how I love Jesus." The stadium was so loud the singing could be heard a mile away. I don't think I have ever seen such a happy crowd as was here in the stadium tonight; they were outdoing the crowds at the football games. We sang about three more songs and then Deacon Bill came to the podium.

Deacon Bill was filled with the spirit tonight. He yelled out, "everyone raise your hands and praise the Lord." About everyone in the stadium had their hands lifted high praising the Lord? Of course there was a few who were weeping because the power of God had fallen on them. And they were under conviction. This would be their night to receive Jesus. After a time of praise Deacon Bill said, "I have an announcement to make.

We will have an afternoon service tomorrow. There will be three portable swimming pools set up to baptize in. The preachers and the deacons will be doing the baptism, some of you lay members can help the people in and out of the pools. There will be dressing rooms set up to change clothes in. Here is what you need to bring: a towel and a complete changing of clothes. If you think you may want to be baptized please bring the clothes and towel. If you have a church home that is preaching the truth, please go there tomorrow morning. Now is everyone ready for tonight's study?" Everyone said amen.

"Tonight we are going to talk about **believer's baptism.** Turn your Bibles to [mark 16: 15, 16] "and he said unto them, go into the all the world and preach the gospel to every creature. He that believeth and is baptized shall be saved; he that believeth not shall be damned." First let's notice to whom he was talking. He was meeting with the eleven apostles after his crucifixion and resurrection and he was commissioning them to go out and spread the gospel to all nations. Of course in their lifetime these eleven would not be able to take the gospel to the entire world, but they would go out win converts, and then commission them to win others until the gospel would be preached around the world. I am sure you took note there was only eleven. Remember Judas had betrayed Jesus and went out and hanged himself leaving eleven apostles. Next let's deal with the gospel, some versions interpret it good news, and truly it is good news. The gospel tells us how to deal with our sinful nature. The apostle Paul later said thru the inspiration of the spirit, [Romans 3:23] "all have sinned and come short of the glory of God" this means we are not living the way God wants us to live. God had put Adam and Eve in a beautiful garden with everything they needed, and he had fellowship with them daily. There was only one thing God asked them not to do. This was not to eat of the tree of knowledge of good and evil, which was in the middle of the Garden of Eden. I think you know the story how Satan enticed them to eat of the tree. When they did they disobeyed God, and when they did God drove them out of the garden, and broke fellowship with them. The Bible teaches we are born in the likeness of Adam. We are born with a sinful nature. We are not a sinner because we commit sin, but we commit sin because we have been born a sinner. We quoted in Romans where Paul said, "All have sinned and come short of the glory of God" then in [Romans 6:23] he said the wages of sin is death. Remember what God said to Adam and eve, "when you eat of the forbidden tree ye shall surely die." Adam and eve didn't die a natural death the moment they ate of the tree, but they died a spiritual death. They no longer had fellowship with God. But God because he loved them devised a plan and that plan would be an animal would be killed as a sacrifice for their sins. It would have to be an animal without spot or blemish. In other words the animal would have to be perfect. God made the first sacrifice when he killed an animal in the garden and clothed them. This sacrifice would continue up through the Old Testament beginning with Abel offering an animal sacrifice. Then Noah's family, Abraham, Isaac, Jacob, Moses, and would continue up to the time when God would give his son [Jesus] on the cross. Then there would be no other sacrifice. Let us read what the writer to the Hebrews said, [Hebrews 9: 12-14] "neither by the blood of goats and calves, but by his [Jesus'] own blood he entered into the holy place, having obtained eternal redemption for us. For if the blood of bulls and goats, and the ashes of a heifer sprinkling the unclean, sanctifieth to the purifying of the flesh: how much more shall the blood of Christ, who through the eternal spirit offered himself without spot to God, purge your conscience from dead works to serve the living God." Jesus said, [John 3:16] "God so loved the world, he gave his only begotten son, that whosoever believeth in him should not perish, but have everlasting life." Jesus said, [John 11:25] "I am the resurrection, and the life: he that believeth in me, though he be dead so shall he live, and whosoever liveth and believeth in me shall never die."

Now lets deal with what Jesus was talking about when he said go into all the world and preach the gospel. The gospel is, we are born a sinner, and we cannot save ourselves, because it takes a perfect sacrifice. Jesus was the perfect sacrifice. The Bible said he who knew no sin became sin for us. Jesus died on the cross-for our sins; he was buried, and rose again on the third day. Forty days later he ascended back to heaven to sit on his father's right hand. There he makes intercession for us. Read "John 3:16 again, "God so loved the world, he gave his only begotten son, that whoever believeth in him should not perish, but have everlasting life." Notice it is not baptism which saves a person, but believing in Jesus' death, resurrection, and ascension.

In acts the eighth Chapter of Acts Phillip was called out on the desert to speak to an Ethiopian Eunuch who was a Jewish convert. He was riding along in his chariot reading Isaiah, a book of prophecy that is in the Old Testament. He was reading this scripture. "He was led as a sheep to the slaughter; and like a lamb dumb before the shearer so opened not his mouth." Philip began at this scripture and preached unto him Jesus! As they rode along they came to some water.

The Eunuch said to Philip "here is water what hinders me to be baptized?"

Philip said, "If you believe with all your heart you may." Notice Philip told the eunuch he would need to believe with all his heart before he was baptized.

In acts the tenth Chapter we have peter preaching to Cornelius a gentile. Peter tells Cornelius about Jesus' life, death, and resurrection. He tells Cornelius in the forty third verse, "that through the name of Jesus. Whosoever believeth in him [Jesus] shall have remission of sins. There are numerous other scriptures that states' believing saves us, but this should be enough to convince anyone that it is the believing that saves us.

Now you may say if believing is what saves us, then why should I be baptized? Because the scriptures teach after a person believes he is to be baptized. Jesus set before us an example by being baptized by John the Baptist, then Jesus said in Marks gospel "he that believeth and is baptized shall be saved." Then he said, "He that believeth not, shall be damned." Take note he didn't say he that is not baptized shall be dammed.

On the day of Pentecost after the Holy Spirit was given, Peter preached a powerful message to the Jews that had crucified Jesus. When they heard this they believed and were pricked in their heart. Then they ask peter what shall we do, and peter tells them, [acts 2:38] "repent, and be baptized every one in the name of Jesus Christ for the remission of sins and ye shall receive the gift of the Holy Ghost." The gift of the Holy Ghost means the Spirit will come in to us giving us a new life. If we read on in the forty-first verse it said, "then they that gladly received his word were baptized: and the same day there was added unto them about three thousand souls." After the eunuch that Phillip had preached to said, he believed with all his heart Phillip baptized him. When Cornelius' believed, all of his family was baptized. When the Philippians Jailer believed in Acts Chapter sixteen he was baptized. Peter said this in [I Peter 3:21] "the like figure whereunto even baptism doth now save us [not the putting away of the filth of the flesh, but the answer of a good conscience toward God, by the resurrection of Jesus Christ." We are saved through Jesus Christ and baptism is the answer to a good conscience, because Jesus said we should do it. So my friends if you have believed, and received Jesus as your savior you should be baptized.

Next we will deal with the proper mode of baptism. The world book encyclopedia states, "early Christians were baptized by emersion or submerged in water." But we shouldn't just take what we have read in the world book encyclopedia but we should go to the word of God.

First let's go to John's baptism. Jesus said it was necessary he be baptized by John. Did John baptize Jesus by emersion, or did he use some other form? First lets read about his baptism in Matthew [Chapter 3:13-16] "then cometh Jesus from Galilee to Jordan unto John to be baptized of him [John the Baptist]. But John forbade him saying, I have need to be baptized of thee, and comest thou to me? And Jesus answering said unto him, suffer it to be so now: for thus it becometh us to fulfill all righteousness. Then he suffered him. And Jesus when he was baptized went straightway up out of the water; and lo, the heavens were opened unto him and he saw the Spirit of God descending like a dove, and light upon him: and lo a voice from heaven saying, this is my beloved Son, in whom I am well pleased." Take note John was baptizing in the Jordan River. Now the gospel of John records the place in the Jordan. [John 3:23] "And John also was baptizing in Aenon near Salim, because there was much water there." Now notice he was baptizing in Aenon because there was much water there. If a person was going to be baptized by pouring or sprinkling it wouldn't take much water. But John must have thought he needed enough water to immerse a person or perhaps he would not have been baptizing there. Now notice another thing in the scripture from Matthew. "And Jesus when he was baptized went up straightway out of the water." I believe this is teaching, when John raised Jesus up from emersion. It was then the Holy Spirit descended upon him like a dove and the voice came from heaven saying this is my beloved son in whom I am well pleased.

Now let's go to the baptism of the eunuch by Philip [Acts 8:38, 39] "and he commanded the chariot to stand still: and they went down into the water both Philip and the eunuch; and he baptized him, and when they were come up out of the water." Notice they went down into the water, and then they came up out of the water.

Now lets go to Paul's writing in [Romans 6:5,6] "for if we have been planted together in the likeness of His death, we shall be also in the likeness of His resurrection: knowing this, that our old man is crucified with him, that the body of sin might be destroyed, that henceforth we should not serve sin." Paul is saying, we have been buried, or planted with him. What does it mean to bury someone? When we bury something don't we cover it up? He said we have been planted. When you plant something don't you cover it up? Paul must mean we are buried with him, in other words we are buried in His likeness. We are planted with Him; we are planted in his likeness. Then Paul said we are resurrected in His likeness. So what is Paul telling us? He is saying when we are baptized by immersion it represents Jesus' death and resurrection. Paul also said in his letter to the Colossian church, "we are buried with him into baptism." I believe we have quoted enough scripture to prove baptism should be by immersion. I have never found any scripture that said there is another way. I know people will say the thief on the cross did not get baptized. That is correct, but the thief did not get the opportunity to be baptized. Remember it is not baptism that saves us, but it represents our new life in Christ. It is an outward expression of an inward change. If you are baptized by immersion without receiving Jesus, you will go down into the water a dry sinner and come out a wet sinner.

Now one more point. If you were to be bitten by a poisonous snake, you are rushed to the hospital. The doctor tells you if you don't soon get an antidote you will die. He said he has two antidotes, he said he is sure one of the antidotes will keep you from death because different ones have testified that it is the right one, but the other one might work but there is nothing in the records saying it will. Which of the antidotes would you choose? I am sure you would choose the one that has been recorded to be the right one.

I would like for you to take this message and ponder it in your heart, if you have received Jesus or will receive Him tonight you need to follow Jesus in baptism. So come tomorrow afternoon with your towel and changing of clothes ready to be baptized.

You have heard the message tonight, we are not saved by baptism, but we are saved through believing the gospel. Accept the fact you are a sinner and cannot save yourself. Realize your sins will lead to eternal death. Believe Jesus took your place on the cross. Receive him into your heart. Then he will honor his word and save you from your sins. Do not put it off until another time. You might not live to see another time. While Brother Robert leads us in a song I am going to ask you to come down front. I will say a prayer with you, and then the counselors will give you instruction on Christian growth. You will leave here a new person in Christ."

Brother Robert begins leading a song of invitation. Then the counselors start down to the front. Those to be saved come down with them. And soon as everyone is down front Deacon Bill leads them in the sinner's prayer, then he turns them over to the counselors for further instructions. Deacon Bill reminds everyone one more time of the Sunday afternoon service, and baptism at 2:00 p.m.

After counseling with two people Stan and Josie have fellowship with other people, and then they leave for home. When they go out of the stadium there are several people carrying signs opposing the services that were being held in the stadium. They are calling the people coming out holy Joes, and saying they are being deceived by Deacon Bill. Some are saying the stadium is government property and should not be used for Christian purposes.

On the way home Stan and Josie talk about what a good spirit there was in the stadium. They also mention the people who were protesting. Josie said, "I believe I have read where Jesus said to pray for our enemies.

"I think you are right," said Stan, "let's pray for them, why don't you pray for them as I drive."

Josie has a prayer for the ones who were protesting. Stan and Josie also talk about them getting baptized on Sunday. They arrive home and crash on the couch and watch a little TV, while they unwind.

Chapter 15

SUNDAY MORNING

Stan and Josie woke up early on Sunday morning. Josie said, "We sure have had an exciting week. First we awoke early in the week and found our children missing which had us disturbed and in sorrow. Then when we began to inquire about them we found the rapture had taken place and we had been left behind. Maria had told me many times the rapture was near, but I didn't pay her much attention, because our Pastor had never mentioned anything about the rapture. Then we met Deacon Bill, who expounded to us more clearly on why we were left behind. We had sure been in the dark about being left behind. Now since we have been listening to Deacon Bill's teachings, repented of our sins and received Christ as our Lord and Savior the Holy Spirit has come in to comfort us and has given us joy and assurance that soon we will be going to be with our children, family, and friends."

"Yes," said Stan, "our lives sure have been changed this week. Jesus has changed our way of thinking, and our attitude about a lot of things, where we work, where we go, what we watch on TV, and to whom we associate with.

Pastor R.B. McCartney

He has turned our sorrow into joy. I have assurance our children are happy today with Jesus".

"Yes," said Josie, "I sure believe the children are with Jesus and I can't wait until our time comes to go there also to be with Jesus and our family and friends. I am going to take my shower, why don't you make the coffee and then I will fix us some breakfast."

"Ok" said Stan, "I will get the coffee on, and then I will shave and shower while you are fixing breakfast."

Josie gets breakfast ready; they turn on the news while they have their breakfast.

The reporter said, "We would like to speak about the revival going on throughout the world. In our country many larger cities are experiencing revival with many people receiving Jesus Christ into their lives. Here in our own city the stadium has been opened up to a Deacon that is having great success in his teaching and convincing the people the rapture has taken place, Jesus has come for those who were ready, and those that weren't living right were left behind. We were there and taped the service last night. We will be viewing the service in a later broadcast.

The stadium was almost filled last night. We could not believe the people could be so joyful, when many of their loved ones had disappeared earlier in the week. Deacon Bill had convinced them their loved ones were gone to heaven and if they would make things right with Jesus they could go and be with them soon.

Last night Deacon Bill spoke on "believer's baptism". He taught we must believe before we are baptized. He said, "We are saved by believing and not by baptism". He also taught, baptism should be by immersion, and only immersion is taught in the Bible. He did give a lot of scripture from the Bible on the subject.

Revival Of Those Left Behind

There were several protesters outside the stadium last night. They were heckling the believers as they left the stadium. They said it was against church and state for the services to be held in the stadium. They said they would be back in force at the Sunday afternoon service. Those coming out of the stadium only said God bless you to the hecklers. I did hear someone say forgive them Lord for they know not what they do.

The ACLU said the services are against the constitution, and they are determined to keep the services from being held in the stadium. They are suing the city, the Mayor, and Deacon Bill in federal court. The court will meet on the issue sometime Monday. We will let you know more about this when it takes place.

At this time we would like to bring you up to date on Bar-Jesus. We talked to our Washington reporter earlier about what is happening in the political world. We will go to our Washington affiliate at this time.

'This is Thomas Novak reporting to you from Washington. We will bring you up to date on the political scene. Bar- Jesus is getting settled into his headquarters in Jerusalem. He is a man that seems to speak with words of power and wisdom. He said he has the solution to end all wars, all poverty, all fraud, and all crime. He is working on a new money system, where everyone will be assigned a number. This will be a secret number on a computer chip so small it can be inserted under the skin. No one else will be able to use this credit card but the one to whom it has been given. This will eliminate all credit card fraud, and because you will not carry any money no one will be able to rob and kill you for your money. Drug dealers and prostitutes will not be able to operate because they will not have the equipment to read your number. There will be a redistributing of wealth around the world eliminating

Pastor R.B. McCartney

hunger. He said, "Because everyone will have everything in common eliminating all jealousy. This will also put a stop to wars. He said he is contacting Bro Luvekin the head of the world church to join him in Jerusalem. He is expected to make a decision any day. He said we are on the way to the greatest times the world has ever known. We will soon be living in paradise. All religions will worship the same God."

I do not know if this is all going to happen or not, but it sure does sound like things in the world are looking up. We do know most of the fighting in the Middle East has stopped for the time being. It is good to not be reporting our boys and girls being killed in war every day. I am sure families who have loved ones in the military are relieved by this good news.

One last thing before we go back to your local station. Bar-Jesus said Mr. Lovekin would be explaining to us soon where all of our loved ones are gone. We will return you to your local news at this time."

Well folks you have heard the report from Washington. It all sounds too good to be true, but I guess we will know more about how it is going to work in a few days. We have been around long enough to know some of the things political leaders promise never come to pass.

Stan and Josie have finished breakfast. They discuss if they are going to Ladoci church on Sunday morning or not. Stan said to Josie, "what do you want to do about church this morning? Do you want to go hear what Pastor Joe has to say, or do you want to stay home and rest and get ready for the afternoon service at the stadium?"

Josie said, "I really think it would be interesting to hear what Pastor Joe is saying about everything that has taken place this past week."

Revival Of Those Left Behind

"Great" said Stan "let's get dressed and go to the second service. I think we will have time after church to stop for fast food and get over to the stadium by service time.

They get dressed and when it is time they head for Ladoci church. As they arrive they notice the parking lot is not as full as usual. "I guess some of the members are late getting here today," said Josie.

"Or maybe they are not coming at all today" said Stan. "They may be sleeping in and going to the stadium this afternoon."

They go inside the church and no one even greets them today. Pastor Joe looks like he is upset; he is thumbing thru a chorus book. The crowd isn't very big. Stan and Josie see someone they know and sit down with them. Josie turns to the lady and said, "What is going on at our church?"

The lady said, "Haven't you heard, many of our people have been going to the Agape Church to hear a Deacon tell what has happened to our loved ones. He is saying Jesus has come and taken them to Heaven, but Pastor Joe said he is just a Deacon in the church which doesn't have any seminary training, and doesn't know what he is talking about. I don't know you guys may have been going to hear him also."

"Yes we have!" Said Josie, "and our lives have been changed this week! We have fully committed our lives to Jesus, and now we are living for him. We believe our children are in heaven with Jesus, and soon we will be going to be with them!"

"Good luck," said the lady I hope you don't get disappointed, but I think you will."

Pastor Joe comes to the podium, and announces he will be leading the praise music this morning in the absence of the music director, and also announces part of the band is missing. He said, "We hope to get everything back in order

Pastor R.B. McCartney

in the next few days, just hang in with us. I always have had a solution and will this time."

The singing wasn't anything to write home about. No one seemed to be in a mood to sing.

Pastor Joe begins his sermon at this time, if you want to call it a sermon. He said, "We have experienced something this week that no one seems to be able to explain. A lot of our love ones have just vanished. Many are saying they have gone to be with Jesus in something they call the rapture. I have challenged them on this because nowhere in the Bible does it mention rapture. They will say rapture means caught out. They are a bunch of false prophets, and one who calls himself Deacon Bill is one of them. He doesn't have any training in being a minister, and is saying those left behind didn't get to go because they had un-confessed sins in their lives. This guy doesn't know anything about the Bible. He is teaching a bunch of lies, and some of you here today have probably been listening to him. Let me set you straight this morning. It doesn't make any difference how you live as long as you believe in Jesus. We are saved because God loved us and sent his son to earth to save us.

Now let us talk about where all our love ones are gone. Do you remember some time back people were talking about UFO's? I am here to tell you those UFO's are real. All these preachers who have been teaching the Lord was coming soon have contacted these beings from outer space and concocted a deal with them to kidnap our love ones and take them to another planet. Of course they moved to this other planet and they are planning on taking over the world soon. They are holding our love ones ransom at this time. We will be hearing from them soon, they will be asking for millions to release our love ones, but when they get the money they will not release our love ones, but will torture and kill them. I think they may get fooled in their plans.

I believe this Bar-Jesus that has come on the scene, as our leader will know how to handle things. He will put these who say they are Christians in their place. He will destroy them with his power and release our love ones back to us. I can hardly wait to see what is going to happen.

Here is something we should all get involved in. The ACLU is suing the city for letting this false prophet, Deacon Bill have services in the stadium. There will be a service at the stadium this afternoon. We want to pray that this will be the last service in the stadium. We also want you to go with us and others there this afternoon in a mass protest against the service. We also want you to go with us to the court house tomorrow to picket while the court is hearing the ACLU's case. If you will help us we can put a stop to the foolishness that is going on. We are going to close the service at this time so you can go get some food and report to the stadium early."

Pastor Joe doesn't have a closing prayer, nor does he go to the back to shake hands with the ones who are leaving.

Stan and Josie talk with some of the people they know on the way out. Some of them were like Stan and Josie they had been going to the services during the week, and listening to Deacon Bill. Stan and Josie ask some of them what they thought about Pastor Joe's sermon.

One lady said, "did you call that a sermon? I cannot believe Pastor Joe can believe the way he does. We have heard the truth from Deacon Bill this week, and now we know that Pastor Joe is a wolf in sheep's clothing. We didn't realize our Pastor was so liberal until this week, and the bad thing about it is he has been leading a lot of us astray. I think he will have to answer to God for his liberal preaching. My husband and I realized this week we never had really been saved. We received Jesus into our lives this week and we are going to be baptized today. We can cope better with our children being missing, since we now have the assurance they are with Jesus."

'Yes", said Josie, "we were just like you guys we thought up to this week everything was ok with our soul. The Bible says all things happen for good to those who love the Lord. I believe after our children were caught out to be with Jesus it has helped us to realize we were lost. We would have still been in our lost condition if the rapture hadn't taken place, and if we didn't go over to hear Deacon Bills' teaching this week. I feel sorry for those who are still walking in sin and being influenced by the devil to believe lies like Pastor Joe is telling. Doesn't Pastor Joe know he is being influenced by the devil to teach the things he teaches?"

"Yes," said the lady, "Pastor Joe has a good education, and has several degrees, but he doesn't seem to know much about the Bible. He doesn't know anything about holy living, he just thinks the Christian can live anyway they want to and be ok. The sad thing about it is he is leading so many people astray, and had led us astray until this week. We know now we shouldn't take mans' word about everything, but we should read our Bibles and check them out

Stan breaks in and said, "Don't you guys think we had better be on our way to the restaurant so we can be on time at the stadium this afternoon. Everyone agrees and they leave.

While Stan and Josie are on their way to the restaurant they discuss the service. Josie said, "Stan I feel sorry for the people of our church. Pastor Joe has deceived the people of our church in believing you can live just any way, and still be a Christian. I wish I could have an opportunity to tell them the truth."

"Yes I feel the same way said Stan, "I thought of a scripture in the Bible where it talks about people learning and not addressing the truth. I think probably our best weapon today would be prayer. Maybe if we pray God will open the door for us to witness to some of them"

"Yes," said Josie, "prayer is a powerful weapon."

They arrive at the restaurant for lunch and go inside for some food. The other couple they were talking with joined them for lunch. They have some good fellowship while they are having their lunch. As soon as they ate lunch both couples head for the stadium.

Chapter 16

BAPTISM AT THE STADIUM

When they arrive at the stadium there is already a large crowd, and the parking lot is beginning to fill up. They get a parking place and head into the stadium. On the way into the stadium there is a large group of protesters. They are calling the people going into the stadium degrading names. Some are spitting at people and trying to block them entering the stadium. Some are trying to provoke a fight. The police are there trying to prevent trouble.

When Stan and Josie get inside there is a complete different atmosphere. Several portable swimming pools have been set up to do the baptismal. Beautiful music is coming over the p.a. system, and the Holy Spirit can be felt throughout the stadium. By two o'clock the stadium is filled to capacity.

Deacon Bill comes to the podium and welcomes everyone to the service. You can tell that he is filled with the spirit by the joy he is expressing. "This has been a wonderful week," he said. "The Bible said the angels rejoice in heaven over the salvation of one lost soul. I am sure they have been

Revival Of Those Left Behind

rejoicing this week, and they haven't been the only ones that have been rejoicing. I have been filled with joy this week and I know there are many of you who have experienced the same joy. It has been a wonderful week and today is a wonderful day. It is going to be great joy to see so many obey the Lord's command to be baptized by emersion. Before we do our baptizing we would like to have prayer and sing a couple of songs."

Deacon Bill prays, Bro Robert comes to the podium and begins to lead everyone in "o how I love Jesus." The singing is so beautiful because everyone seem to be singing in the spirit. Bro Robert then leads out the song "He is Lord." Now about everyone has their hands raised to the sky, their eyes turned toward heaven and is shedding tears of joy. Several are saying hallelujah praise the Lord. Some are saying glory to God, and some are saying thank you Jesus.

Deacon Bill comes back to the podium he is filled with such joy, and is saying praise the Lord. This is all he can say for awhile. When he finally comes down from the mountain top he begins to talk about the baptism. He said, "We have several others which will be helping us do the baptism. If you have received Jesus into your heart and want to be baptized we are going to ask you to gather around the pools. Make one line going into each pool. Steps have been set up on the west side of the pools to go into the pools. When you get into the pool go directly to someone who is available. Then when you are baptized the one who baptizes you will direct you to the east side to go out. Some of you that are being baptized can help others in and out of the pool. One pool has been set up with a ramp for those who are handicapped and in wheel chairs.

We will pray at this time, and then we will make our way to the pools. Father it is a joy to come to this part of our service, with so many going down into the water to be buried

Pastor R.B. McCartney

with you into baptism. They are being buried representing your death, and being raised into newness of life representing your resurrection from the dead. We pray each one that is baptized today might walk worthy of you. We realize each of us is going to be tested in the days to come. We know according to scripture and what is already happening on the world scene Christians are going to be persecuted, so Lord help us all to stand strong in you. In Jesus name we pray."

"I would point out to you at this time if you haven't invited Jesus into your heart you need to do that before you are buried with Him in baptism, because if you haven't repented of your sins, and received Jesus into your heart you are still a sinner. You will just go into the water a dry sinner and come out a wet sinner. This water here today has no saving power, but it represents the death of the old sinner you were, being buried in a watery grave and being raised a new man Before we begin the baptism we wish to invite those who haven't received Jesus to do so at this time. If you haven't received Jesus please step out from your seat at this time and come down to the platform."

Several people get up and come forward for prayer. Deacon Bill prays with them to receive Jesus, and then Deacon Bill tells them to go over to the pools and get in front of the line to be baptized. He tells the other people being baptized to let them be first as they haven't brought towels or changing of clothes they will have time to dry off while the others are being baptized.

He said, "The rest of you to be baptized will now make your way to the pools."

The field is filled with people, the pools are filled with people being baptized, the spirit of the Lord is filling the stadium, and it is a joyful time for everyone in the stadium. The baptism lasts for three hours, but no one seems to be bored or tired.

When everyone is baptized Deacon Bill comes back to the podium. He said, "We estimate there has been over three thousand baptized this afternoon. Let's hear everyone give a great shout, "glory to God." The crowd could be heard for miles. Deacon Bill said, "You would think our team had just won the World Series, and really it has and more than the World Series, I think we have won the Universal series with angels as our cheer leaders, and Jesus as our coach. Let's give the Lord a good applause." Everyone joins together in a loud applause.

Deacon Bill said, "We have had a wonderful afternoon, in fact we have had a quite a week. It started off with sorrow, but has ended up with joy. I believe revival has been going on throughout the world this week. I have heard people talk about great revival at the time of the end, and I believe this is it. But now the bad news we are not sure if the stadium will be available to us tomorrow night. I am sure you have heard the ACLU is saying we are violating the constitution of the United States by having services in the stadium. They say it is against Church and state. They are going before a federal judge tomorrow trying to block the services. They have also contacted Mr. Bar-Jesus asking him to make a world wide proclamation on religion. If they are successful we will not be allowed to have services tomorrow night.

Here is one thing I think I should address this evening in case we are not allowed to have any more services after today. Mr. Bar-Jesus has already been talking about setting up a new money system. If this is what it sounds like, it could be the mark of the beast as described in [Revelation 13:14-17] "he said to them who dwell on the earth that they should make an image to the beast, which has a wound from the sword, and did live. And he hath power to give life to the image of the beast that the image of the beast should both speak, and because that as many as would not worship the image of the beast should be killed. And he caused all, both small and great, rich and poor, free and bond, to receive a mark in their right hand, or in their foreheads: and no man might buy or sell, save he that had the mark or the name of the beast, or the number of his name," so what ever you do don't take the mark or your destiny will be sealed. You will be rejecting Jesus and receiving the antichrist. I am sure there will be some who will say "God will understand if I receive the mark so we can have food."

This is similar to what many were saying before the rapture. They were saying, "You can live a sinful life and still go in the rapture." A lot of us made that mistake. Here is what God said will happen to those who take the mark. [Revelation 14:9-11] "And the third angel followed them, saying with a loud voice, if any man worship the beast and his image, and receive his mark in his forehead, or in his hand. The same shall drink of the wine of the wrath of God, which is poured out with out mixture into the cup of his indignation; and he shall be tormented with fire and brimstone in the presence of the holy angels, and in the presence of the lamb: [Jesus] and the smoke of their torment ascended up for ever and ever: and they have no rest day or night, who worship the beast and his image, and whosoever recieveth the mark of his name."

Now here is what I ask you to do. When you get home tonight get on your knees and pray like you have not prayed before. Be real truthful with God let him know you are going to be faithful to him, and will serve him and no other Gods. Make up your mind that you will not worship the image of the beast or take his mark. Settle it in your heart and stick to it.

Tune in tomorrow afternoon to the local television station for instruction on tomorrow nights service. It will be announced if we can have a service.

Revival Of Those Left Behind

One last thing before we leave for our homes. I have been told there are many protesters outside. Do your best to act as a Christian and not let their heckling get next to you. Just remember the words of Jesus. "If they persecute me they will persecute you also." Good night and May God bless each of you as you go.

Stan and Josie are not in any hurry to go home. They share with others what a great day it is and what a wonderful blessing it has been to be baptized. They see the Mcelliots they are bubbling with joy. They have also been baptized. They share for a while, and then they decide to go home. They walk out of the stadium together. The protesters are there in number, they are heckling those leaving and calling them names.

Guess who they see, yes it is Pastor Joe. He calls them turn coats, and tells them they are heretics to the faith, and will soon find out what Deacon Bill is teaching is a lie. He said their bubble is about ready to burst, and he is doing everything in his power to see that it does.

Josie said, "I am sorry you feel that way Pastor Joe, we still love you and wish you could believe the truth."

Pastor Joe speaks with anger in his heart and said, "I do believe the truth. It is you guys who are being deceived."

Stan said, "Come Josie lets go home it is no time to discuss these things with Pastor."

When they get out to the parking lot Mr. Mcelliot said, "It is really amazing what has taken place in my life. A few days back I would have punched some of those protesters in the nose, now I have compassion for them knowing they are letting the devil deceive them.

"Yes," said Stan I would have probably done the same thing." After they have shared the blessings of Jesus with one another for a while Stan said, "Why don't we stop at a restaurant and have dinner. We can continue our fellowship there."

"Sounds good to me said Mr. Mcelliot."

Josie and Mrs. Mcelliot agree. They head for the restaurant. The restaurant is crowded because many others have stopped for dinner. The hostess seats them at a table, and it is the last table left in the restaurant.

A man at the table next to theirs had been drinking and he was rather loud. He was yelling at the waitress, and wanting to know why he isn't getting better service. She tells him they are busier tonight than usual because of the service letting out at the stadium. Then he really gets loud and begins to curse saying, "the people attending those services are all a bunch of crazy lunatics. They are saying someone named Jesus has come for their loved ones and taken them to Heaven. They are crazy to believe in someone called Jesus. I don't believe in all of this foolishness. I don't believe in a Heaven or a hell. He looks over at Stan and said you don't believe in all that foolishness do you?"

Stan said, "Yes I really do, and He has changed our lives, and He would like to change yours."

"Baloney," said the guy; "I believe I saw you working down at the casino the other day. He looks at Josie and said, and you were serving drinks to me."

"Yes" said Stan, "that was the other day, but today we have a new life. We went forward this week in the meetings; repented of our sins, invited Jesus into our lives, and He has changed our way of thinking. Josie and I have quit the casino, and went to work at the hospital. We have begun living for the Lord. The Holy Spirit has come into our lives, and is leading us in all that we do. Our children have gone to be with Jesus, and we are determined to go be with them in Heaven."

Mr. Mcelliot speaks up and said, "Yes Jesus has made a change in my wife and me this week. We didn't think we had to go to church to be a Christian but when we awoke with our children missing this week, we heard through Stan and Josie a Deacon named Bill was teaching from the Bible and had convinced them Jesus had come for His church and taken all the children, and the adults that were living for Him to Heaven. We went to listen to him and decided he was teaching the truth. The Holy Spirit begins to speak to us about receiving Jesus. We went forward and received Jesus as our savior. The Holy Spirit came into our lives and we were born again. We have become a new creation in Christ"

Josie and Mrs.Mcelliot said, "Praise the Lord!"

The man said, "You guys seem like you really have made a change this week." He begins to shed tears and say, "my wife has left me because of my drinking, and abuse. She and My children are also missing. I did love them very much, but had let my drinking destroy my marriage. I have heard about the revival going on at the stadium, and a voice would tell me I needed to check it out, but another voice would tell me to act like a man. He said only people who were weaklings would attend services like that. It was Satan speaking through me before when I said I didn't believe in God. That was just a front I was putting on. I do believe in God. I do believe in a Heaven and a hell, and I don't believe I would go to Heaven if I were to die this night. I don't want to go to hell. Can you guys tell me how I can go to Heaven?"

"Sure" said Stan. "Why don't you join us here at our table?"

"Ok thanks," he said and pulls up a chair at their table and said, "by the way my name is Henry." They introduce themselves to him also.

Pastor R.B. McCartney

By this time they all have their food, and begin to eat while they talk.

Stan said, "Henry, what do you know about Jesus, have you ever read the Bible?"

"Yes" said Henry, "my mother took me to Sunday school when I was young. I learned there about Jesus dieing on the cross for our sins, but I never did invite Him into my heart. After I got older I quit going to Sunday school. I was too busy with other things."

Stan said, "Henry you said you didn't believe you would go to heaven if you died tonight. Let me ask you this question, are you a sinner?"

"Sure" said Henry, "I know I am a sinner."

Stan said, "Do you believe Jesus died on the cross for your sins?"

"Yes," said Henry, "I do believe that He did"

"Ok" said Stan, "I will explain to you how the Bible said we can be saved.

Number one; we must hear the word; this would be thru preaching, teaching, or by studying the Bible. Thru the word we realize we are a sinner, and only through Jesus can we have our sins forgiven. The next step is repentance. Repent means to regret we have broken Gods laws, and have a desire to change our way of living. The next step is believing. We must believe Jesus died on the cross for our sins; in other words He took the punishment we deserved. The next step is receive Jesus into our heart. When these four things take place within our heart, if we are sincere in all of these the Holy Spirit comes into our lives and begins the process of making us a new person in Christ.

Henry you have already said you have heard the word and admit that you are a sinner. Do you desire to change the way you have been living?"

Henry begins to weep and said, "Yes I want my life to change, I want to receive Jesus into my heart tonight."

"Ok, said Stan I will ask you to bow your head and repeat this prayer after me. Dear Lord I realize I am a sinner.

I know I cannot save myself.

I repent of my sins.

I believe you died for my sins.

I invite you into my life to be my Lord.

I will do my best to live for you from now on. Amen.

If you meant this prayer with all your heart you have become one of Gods children. You have become a new creation in Christ. You are now a baby in Christ. Babies must be fed to grow, so now you need to be fed the word of God. The more you study the word, pray and attend church the more you will grow in the Lord. Then you also need to follow the Lord in baptism. This will represent the death of the sinner you were, the burial, and then the resurrection of a new man from the grave."

Henry is still weeping, and said, "I really meant business with God, and intend to serve Him with all of my heart". He begins to hug everybody at the table, and say "I love you all with all of my heart, thank you for sharing Jesus with me tonight." Everyone at the table are weeping and praising God.

Some of the people at the other tables are giving thumbs up, but there are others who act if they are getting offended.

After they share for awhile they decide its time to head for home. They all say bye and head for their separate homes. Stan and Josie are on cloud nine because they have led someone to accept Christ.

When Stan and Josie arrive home Stan said, "I think tonight instead of watching the TV. I am going to study the Bible."

"Yes" said Josie, "I think that is a good idea, I am going to do the same. Why don't we study the same place? Then we could ask each other questions when we read a Chapter."

"Sounds great" said Stan, "shall we study the Book of John?"

"Sounds good to me," said Josie.

They study for awhile, have prayer together and turn in for the night.

Chapter 17

MESSAGE FROM THE PRESIDENT

It seems like morning came too early for Stan and Josie. Neither of them is ready to get up, but they are anxious to hear the morning news to see if there has been anything developing over night.

They have had quite a week. First they had much sorrow when they awoke early in the week to find their children missing. When they began to search the neighborhood they found they weren't the only ones which had loved ones missing, and the news was reporting the world to be in chaos because of people missing from cars, trucks, buses, trains, ships, and airplanes causing accidents all over the world. Everything was in a disastrous state. The news was saying that some people were saying the rapture of the church had taken place and Jesus had come for those, who were ready. Others were reporting aliens from another planet had carried the missing ones away to another planet.

Stan and Josie had gone to the Ladoci church to see if their pastor knew anything about what had taken place. He didn't know what had happened, but did have some of his relatives missing also. He had assured them Jesus had not come for the church, and the Bible didn't mention anything about a rapture Stan and Josie had decided to go over to the Agape Church where Maria attended to see if their pastor knew anything. When they arrived there they found their pastor was missing and many of the church members were also missing. They had met a Deacon by the name of Bill who told them he was certain Jesus had come and they had all been left behind. This meeting was the start of a city wide revival, which had been sweeping the city with record attendance. The revival had started in the Agape Church, which soon was overcrowded and had been moved to the stadium. Many people had received Jesus into their heart, or rededicated their lives to Jesus. Many of the people had been going to churches that weren't preaching the gospel, and never had been born again. Today they would be anxious to find out if there would be a service in the stadium tonight, because the ACLU was suing the city to stop the services.

Stan gets out of bed first and goes to the kitchen and puts on a pot of coffee. Josie comes behind him and turns on the news and starts breakfast. Stan relaxes in a chair to listen to the news and wait for the coffee to get ready. The local reporter is reporting the news happening around the country. He talks about thousands being saved around the world in the greatest revival the world had known in many years. He talks about the large baptismal service which had taken place at the stadium yesterday and had shown it live on TV. And then he said not everyone is happy over the revivals. He said there are millions of people throughout the world protesting the revivals, and saying there hasn't been any thing like the rapture of the church taking place, and those going around teaching Jesus has come and taken the church to heaven are just a bunch of liars and are deceiving many people. Some of them are very angry and are trying to antagonize those who say the rapture has taken place to fight with them. Some have been hitting, and spitting on those who talk about a revival taking place, but those who are Christians are turning the other cheek. The protesters are asking the ACLU to do something to stop the revival. The court will hear the ACLU today on the issue of having the Christian services in our stadium, which they say is violating the constitution of the USA.

At this time we will go to Washington DC where the President is about to address the nation."

"Good morning to you who have joined us from around the nation. We are standing by for the President. He will be out any minute to address the nation. Here comes the President now."

The President comes to the podium and begins to address the nation. "Good morning fellow Americans. I have been your President for only a short time. I have already found out I have a big job on my hands and I am going to need your help as we try to get our nation up and running. The things that took place this past week has caused chaos throughout our nation. There has been some progress, but we have a long way to go getting back to normal. Many of our rail lines are still closed down. Crews are working overtime to get them up and running. Our highway system still has several problems. Some bridges are requiring much reconstruction, and will be some time before they will be opened for traffic.

There are a few airports that are still closed because of damage to their control towers, or damage to the terminals. Most of our factories are running behind on production. Hospitals are still crowded because of those who have been wounded in accidents. Some rooms were made available on the day the rapture took place when some of the patients just vanished from their rooms. There seems to be plenty homes for people to live in since many were made vacant on the day of the rapture by people who disappeared. There is a teacher shortage in some of our high schools, but we are solving this problem by moving our elementary teachers to teaching jobs in our high schools. Many of our elementary schools in lower grades will be closed because of the lack of students. This job before me is more than I can handle alone; I plan to spend much time on my knees asking almighty God to help us. I think with the help of God, and your help we can work together to return things back to normal

Here is what I need you to do, first of all pray for us, and then I need you to give your best in the weeks to come. It may mean changing your life style so as to do a better job where you work. In some cases it may mean changing jobs and working long hours. I know some of you have been involved in a great revival this week and many of you have repented of your sins and made things right with the Lord. I also have made things right with the Lord. I will not ask you to do anything that will not please our Lord, but here is what I am asking you to do. Those that are having teaching sessions during the week, I am going to ask you to begin to have meetings on the weekend, Saturday through Sunday night. This will allow everyone to produce better productivity on their jobs in order to get our country running smoothly again. If you will do this for us, and the good of our wonderful country it will be appreciated. But please don't neglect to find some time to pray. It is very important to talk to God each day. May God bless everyone and may we each do our part."

The Washington reporter said, "We will have comments on the President's speech later in the day. I am sure we will hear from the Senate and Congress a little later. At this time we will return you to your local station."

Revival Of Those Left Behind

When the news returns to the local station Stan said to Josie, "we had better hurry or we will be late for work at the hospital." As soon as they can get ready they get on their way to the hospital. On the way they talk about the President's speech. Josie said to Stan, "what did you think about the President's speech?"

Stan said, "I think he is right on in the things he said. I do not think he gave a political speech, I think he was speaking from his heart on what everyone needs to do for our country, and I liked the part where he said he would have to stay on his knees asking God to help him in his decisions. It is unusual for a politician to mention getting on their knees in prayer in this liberal society we are living in."

"Yes," said Josie, "I thought he was right on. I know we have been having a good time in the services this past week and I hate to miss a night of Deacon Bill's teaching. But I guess some of the people who have night jobs were missing work so as not to miss any of his teachings. I can't blame them for that, as I know we wouldn't have wanted to miss a night, and I think the hospital was having a shortage of workers on the night shift. Of course I realize not all the help at the hospital were interested in any gospel services, but some were interested to hear what had happened to everyone."

"Yes," said Stan, "some were interested but they didn't believe the missing people had been caught out to Heaven. I think they believed those missing had been kidnapped by someone."

Stan and Josie arrive at work. Stan gives Josie a kiss, and said; "I will see you in the break room at lunch."

"Sure thing" said Josie, "maybe the court will have ruled on whether the services can continue in the stadium. As soon as they do I am sure Deacon Bill will be speaking."

"Sure thing," said Stan," see you at noon."

At noon they meet in the lunch room to watch the news. They had already heard bits and pieces of the decision the federal judge had handed down and it did sound good. The news was coming on just as they entered the lunch room, and the top story would be the ruling on religious services being held in the stadium.

Ann was reporting. She said, "The federal judge has made the ruling that the services may continue in the stadium. We are going to listen to his entire ruling as we take you by audio that we recorded earlier in his court room. Listen as we play the tape."

"It is this courts ruling that the religious services being held in the stadium is not a violation of the constitution of the United States. We will explain to you how we came to this conclusion. First let's read the first amendment to the constitution of the United States. "Congress shall make no law respecting an establishment of religion, or prohibit the free exercise thereof; or abridge the freedom of speech, or the press; or the right of the people peaceably to assemble, and to petition the government for a redress of grievances." We do not see anything in this amendment to say religious speech cannot go on in public property or people cannot assemble to listen to religious speech. Let us take this one thing at a time. **"Congress shall make no law respecting an establishment of religion, or prohibit the free exercise thereof."** Does this say our nation wants freedom of religion or freedom from religion? I believe if we study the history of the early pioneers and law makers that came to our country they were seeking freedom of worship. They had come from a land where they did not have freedom to worship as they pleased. If they were caught teaching contrary to the doctrine of the established church they were put to death. Then after they came to this country, there were those that had come to this country, which wanted to limit the people to their religion, and wanted the state to establish their religion as the only one making it a state run religion. This is what prompted congress to make a ruling on freedom of religion. This said nothing about not being able to meet, speak, or pray in any government or public building as long as it is scheduled according to not hinder other things that have been scheduled. Now let's go to the part about freedom of speech. Let's read what it said; "**or abridge the freedom of speech.**" Do you see anything here that would prohibit the religious people their right of freedom to speak? Look at the next one on assembly, "**or the right of the people to peacefully assemble.**" I do not see anything here to say religious people cannot assemble in or on government property as long as they do it peacefully. Therefore we rule the services may go on in the stadium as long as it does not conflict with the other activities scheduled in the stadium. That is my ruling, thank you very much."

The reporter said, "You have heard the ruling of the court. Many people are rejoicing, but on the other hand many are upset over the ruling and the ACLU said they will appeal to a higher court. We do not know yet about the service tonight that will be up to Deacon Bill's decision. He does know what the President has requested, and we think he will go along with the request of the President. We are told he is on his way down to the station at this time. So as soon as he arrives we will hear from him. Hold for a minute here is Deacon Bill coming into the studio at this time. Good afternoon Deacon Bill, we are glad you could come down and let people know what is going to happen with the services, or have you had time to make that decision?"

"Yes Ann, I have made a decision. After listening to the President speak this morning I begin to contact God in prayer to help me make the right decision if the federal

Pastor R.B. McCartney

judge were to rule in our favor. I also called our Mayor and got his opinion. His thoughts were we should go along with the President. After much prayer, I believe God spoke to me through his word. I read where we are under the authority of those who rule over us. I believe it is saying as long as their ruling doesn't conflict with our Christian beliefs. I believe what the President requested was for the betterment of our people, and the President was expressing love for his fellow man when he made the request. I believe our President is a Godly man. I was thrilled when he talked about asking God to help him make decisions.

Here is my decision: I am thrilled with the decision the federal judge has made this day. We have seen Christianity ruled out of anything that might be connected with city, county, state, or federal government. It would appear our country would like to have freedom from religion, instead of freedom of religion. Some liberal judges had made up their own constitution. I believe we are now on the road to restore our freedom that our forefathers had intended when they established the constitution of the United States. I believe this is one of the happiest days of my life. We will gladly go along with our President and help get our country up and running again. We will begin having two services on Saturday, Saturday afternoon at 2:00 p.m., and another service on Saturday night at 7:00 p.m. On Sunday we will have one service at 2:00 p.m. We urge everyone, read your Bible daily, and pray. Don, t forget, no service tonight, but we will look forward to seeing you on Saturday, and Sunday. Thank you Ann for allowing me to speak."

"Yes, and thanks for coming down to our studio. I am sure this has answered the question everyone has been anxious to hear. We will be announcing your decision throughout the afternoon."

Stan and Josie are excited over the ruling. They are praising God in the lunch room, but some people are giving them hard looks as if they are about ready to tackle them.

Josie looks at her watch and said, "Stan we had better get back to work."

"Yes," he said. "It is about that time. I will see you after work."

"Ok," said Josie, "don't work too hard."

Stan and Josie get off from work and start home. Stan said to Josie "how would you like to stop at a restaurant for dinner? I think we should celebrate the decision that the court has handed down this day. It has been several years since the courts have handed down a ruling in favor of religion."

"Yes," said Josie, "you are absolutely right, and I am ready to celebrate. I didn't have anything planned to cook for tonight, and besides we haven't done much grocery shopping the past week. So I don't think we have anything to cook. We better stop after dinner and get some groceries."

The restaurant is not very crowded, so they get seated right away, and order dinner. The TV is on and they are viewing the evening news. The top news is about the President's speech, and the court ruling in favor of the church. Most of the people in the restaurant seem to be happy about the ruling, but there is a few which seems to be upset and are showing it by their language, and loudness. Josie overhears the conversation at the table next to them. They are talking about the court decision and the revival, which is taking place around the world. They seem to be very happy over what is taking place. Josie said to them, "you guys must be Christians."

"Yes!" Said the lady "Would you guys like to sit with us during dinner?"

Josie looks at Stan. Stan said, "Sure why not."

Stan and Josie join them at their table, introduce themselves to them and they introduce themselves as Sam and Jan and begin to talk about the things that had taken place the past week. Sam was an airline pilot, and was on a flight from Korea to Los Angeles. He begins to tell some of the things that took place on the flight.

He said, "It was a normal flight, weather was good, we were about two hours out from Los Angeles when I begin to hear screams coming from the cabin. I turned to the co-pilot to tell him to check what was going on. He was gone! I was baffled; I knew he had not gone back to the cabin, because I would have known if the cockpit door had opened. I called to one of the flight attendants and asked him what was going on."

He said, "I am not sure but we have several passengers missing from the plane. All of the cabin doors are secure, and we have one flight attendant missing. It is a little weird. There isn't a small child left on the plane. Where has everyone disappeared too, there is no place to hide on the plane. One lady said she knows what has taken place. She said, some of her friends have been telling her Jesus was coming soon, and if she didn't confess Jesus she would be left behind."

"By this time my radio was going wild. Planes were going down all over the world; some control towers could not be reached. Others were reporting planes going down everywhere. Some had crashed on landing. I reached the tower at Los Angeles on my radio. He said things were in a mess there. I put things together and then I knew Jesus truly had come. My co-pilot was what I had called a radical Christian. He was always trying to witness to me. The wife and I attended church once and awhile, usually Christmas or Easter, but we never got involved in anything at the church. I don't think the pastor even knew our names. But

I did remember one Sunday pastor had talked about Jesus coming for the church, and he said he thought it would be soon.

I was able to reach the wife on the phone, she was pretty shook up, she was crying and said the children were missing, and she wished I were there. I told her I would be landed in two hours if things went well, and would come straight home. I wasn't able to land at Los Angeles International, but they landed me at Edwards out on the desert. They had a clear runway there. I made my way home as soon as possible and found the wife was still shook up, but so was I.

We listened to every news station we could find. We were like everyone else trying to find out what was going on, and where our loved ones that had disappeared were at. After a couple of days passed by and different people were giving their ideas what had happened. I told my wife I really believed it had something to do with the Lord, and we agreed and begin to try to pray. Then we heard about a Deacon named Bill who was teaching at the Agape Church saying Jesus had come for the church, and was giving scripture to prove it. We started attending that day, got on our knees and asked Jesus to come into our hearts. We haven't been the same since then. We believe our children are with Jesus."

"Yes," said Jan, "even though our children are missing the Holy Spirit has filled our heart with joy. And we feel they are just a prayer away, and we are going to be with them soon. We were both baptized yesterday and are happier than we have been in a long time."

Stan and Josie share with them their conversion, and baptism the past week. They share awhile longer and head for the super market for groceries. When they get home they share some things about work during the day. Josie checks the computer and they have an e-mail from Deacon Bill saying the revival will continue on Saturday, and he would like to meet with the workers Thursday night at 7:00 o'clock P.M. at the Agape Church. She asks Stan if that will be ok, he said yes. She sends Deacon Bill a note back and said ok they will be there. They spend some time reading the Bible, and praying then they turn in early for the night.

Chapter 18

THE REVIVAL CONTINUES

When Stan and Josie get home from work on Tuesday night Josie calls the Mcelliots and invites them over for a time of fellowship, up until now they had been too busy working and attending the revival to have very much fellowship together.

Mr. Mcelliot said, "Sure, what time would you like us to come over."

"Would seven be ok for you guys," said Josie.

"Sounds good," said Mr. Mcelliot, "we will see you then."

Josie prepares dinner. She and Stan have dinner, after dinner they watch some news on television. The news is still talking about the revival that is going on. They also mention the court ruling on Monday, but they also mention that the ACLU is appealing to the Supreme Court, and they will probably hear the case before the week is out.

The Mcelliots arrive. Josie gives them a big hug and tells them to have a seat. Mr. Mcelliots said, "I think since we have become such good friends in the past week you guys should begin to call us by our first name. I know up to now you have only known us by our last name. My name is Bob and the wife's name is Susan, but she prefers to be called Sue."

"Sure," said Stan, "I think it is about time. We have been neighbors for a long time but never got to know each other very well. We were doing our thing and you guys were doing yours. Of course you were always friendly when we spoke to you, and we tried to be friendly also. It wasn't because we didn't like you guys for neighbors, but we were all busy with our family, and you were busy with yours."

"Yes" said Bob, "we saw you guys going to church on Sunday and we thought you guys thought you were better than us, but since the kids went to be with Jesus we have found out that you didn't.

"Yes" said Sue, "Bob had become so bitter against churches. He thought the preachers were all out to get our money. We wanted to keep our distance because we were afraid you guys would try to get us to go to church. We didn't want our children to get too close to your children in fear they would try to get them to go to church. Thank God you guys did invite us to go with you last week. The children being missing made the difference."

"Yes," said Bob, "and what a difference it has made. If Jesus had not come for our children we would have still been lost in our sins, and thank God for you guys inviting us to hear Deacon Bill. We owe our gratitude to you guys for inviting us, but most of all we owe our gratitude to Jesus for receiving us into his fellowship, and forgiving us for rejecting him for so long. We have a new life in him now. What a difference he has made in our lives."

Stan said, "We knew when we would leave for church on Sunday if you were out in the yard you would act like you didn't see us. You can see it turned out we were no better than you guys. We got left behind just like you guys. Yes, we went to church and we were religious, but we didn't have salvation. The Lord said in Isaiah, "this people draw close to me with their lips, but their heart is far from me." This was the category we were in until this past week. We went to church on Sunday, we sang the songs, prayed the prayers, acted like we were holy, but never had invited Jesus into our heart. I would say we were just religious and that was about it. We professed but didn't possess. We were no better than you guys."

"Yes," said Josie, "only I was probably a little worse. I had this friend Maria that kept telling me our pastor wasn't preaching the word, and we needed to get into a church that preached the word, but I wouldn't listen to her. Sometimes she really bugged me and I would tell her to butt off, but I sure wish I had listened to her. If I had I would be up there where she is today and I would have been with our children. I think if I would have gone to another church Stan would have probably gone with me."

"Well I don't know about that," said Stan, "I was pretty comfortable going to Pastor Joe's church, and he was a smooth talker. I really thought we were living the Christian life, but sure found out different this past week. But I guess we shouldn't be looking back, but start looking at the future.

"Yes" said Bob, "I thank God I am not what I used to be. I heard this expression one time, and I think it fits us all pretty good.

I am not what I ought to be.

I am not what I am going to be.

But thank God I am not what I used to be."

"Yes" said Sue, "I am glad we are not what we used to be. I have joy now that I never had before. I didn't know Jesus could make such a difference in our lives. When I awoke last week and the children were gone. I thought I would never be happy again. Even though some were saying our children were happy in heaven with Jesus, that didn't give me much comfort, but since I invited Jesus into my life it has made all the difference. I have assurance now we will see them again, and soon."

"Yes," said Josie, "I don't think it is going to be very long. Even if it were a long time I would not want to bring them back to this sinful world. There are too many bad things going on in this world, and too many things to lead the children astray.

"Forgive me," said Josie, "I didn't ask you guys if you would like something to drink. We have coke, tea, coffee, and water. We were so busy sharing I just forgot."

"That's ok," said Bob, "I don't think anyone was really thirsty, and besides we didn't come to stay long as we all have to go to work tomorrow. I think we will skip the drink at this time. We need to be going home. I have to get out early tomorrow."

"We have enjoyed your visit," said Stan, "I hope we can get together more often. I just thought of something, did you guys get an e-mail from Deacon Bill about the meeting for workers Thursday night? I thought we could probably all ride together."

"Yes, we sure did," said Bob, "we will be happy to ride together. We can take our car if you like."

Stan said, "We can go in ours, or yours. I guess we can decide Thursday night. How about us praying together before you guys leave?"

"Sure," said Bob, "we need all the prayer we can get."

They have prayer together. After prayer Bob and Sue leave for home, Stan and Josie recline in their chairs for a while to relax before going to bed. After a while they become sleepy and decide to turn in for the night.

Thursday night comes. Stan and Josie get home from work; they have stopped for fast food on the way home.

They call Bob and Sue. Bob said he will take his car to the meeting, and they agree to leave around 6:30. Stan and Josie freshen up and get ready. They meet over at Bob and Sue's house and they are on the way. When they get to Agape Church Deacon Bill greets them with a hug, and said, "The meeting will start as soon as everyone arrives." While they are waiting they tell Deacon Bill how much they appreciated his teachings the past week and how their lives have been changed. Deacon Bill tells them how much it has meant to him and how God has blessed him.

After everyone arrives they begin the meeting. After Deacon Bill tells everyone how much he appreciates them coming out for the meeting he said, "before we go any farther with our meeting we would like to go to the Lord Jesus in prayer to thank Him for all he has done for us this past week. He has done things for us we didn't really deserve. He had been warning all of us in past years to get our hearts ready to meet him, but we had all ignored what he was saying to us through the Holy Spirit. We had grieved his Holy Spirit and trampled his blood under our feet. If he would have given us what we deserve we all would be on our way to a burning hell, and lake of fire, but thanks be to God, he believes in a second chance. Lets pray." Deacon Bill prays a very powerful prayer. You could tell he was praying in the spirit. He wasn't praying for God to give us anything, but he was thanking him for his goodness and mercy. After prayer Deacon Bill begins to speak from his heart.

"Brothers and sisters we have just had a wonderful week. It started off being the worse week any of us had ever experienced, but we didn't realize God was at work. God said in [Romans 8:28] "we know that all things work together for good to them that love God, to them who are the called according to his purpose." When we awakened the other morning finding some of our family members missing, we thought we were having one of the worse night mares we had ever experienced. We didn't realize God was working out everything according to his plan, and it would be for our good. Most of us weren't giving much thought to where we would spend eternity if we were to die that very day, but when we awakened to find our loved ones missing we began to inquire where they were. I know some of you were almost in a panic state, but as we all began to search the scriptures, Gods' plan began to come into focus. We realized the rapture had taken place, and we had been left behind. Gods' plan was right on schedule He had come for his bride, and we had been left behind. I began to seek God like never before but I began to realize if I wanted to see my family again I would have to live for the Lord from here on until he would call me home. The scripture [Romans 8:28] has more meaning for me today. I realize if I hadn't been left behind I would not have been able to teach all of you this past week. I am not saying God left me behind for this purpose. He left me behind because I had sin in my life and kept on sinning, but since I was left behind He used me for His purpose.

Now let us talk about the services to continue in the stadium. We have much joy because of the decision that was handed down by the court this week, but we do not know how much longer we will be able to meet in the stadium. It is possible the Supreme Court will rule in our favor, but I think this Bar-Jesus will soon rule out any services that will teach the rapture of the church has taken place. I think these liberal Churches will pressure him to shut down any church which is teaching the rapture, and I don't think it will be long until he sets up the mark of the beast to be able to buy or sell. I think you all know God forbids any Christian from taking the mark. You may read in Revelation Chapter fourteen what God said.

Revival Of Those Left Behind

Bar-Jesus has already mentioned the chip to stop credit card thief, and to many it will sound good. If Bar-Jesus is the antichrist to come on the scene as described in Revelation chapter 13, here is what we believe will happen in the next seven years. Revelation [13:7] says, "it was granted to him [antichrist] to make war with the saints and to overcome them." We believe there will be some nations that will not sign an agreement with the antichrist. We do not know if the United States will be one of those nations that will buy into his plan or not, but if they do not, the Antichrist and those Nations who have joined his league will declare war on the United States immediately and all those who haven't taken his mark will be hunted down and killed. But this will not just happen in the United States, but he will declare war against Christian throughout the world. In Revelation [chapter 6:7, 8] we read where one fourth of the earth's population is destroyed by Sword, hunger, and death by the beast. [antichrist]

We believe communist nations like China, Russia, and other communist nations will sign an agreement at first with the antichrist and receive the mark to be able to buy and sell, but when he stands in the temple and declares himself to be god they will break their league with him, and the world will be plunged into a nuclear war leading up to the battle of Armageddon, described in the trumpet judgments described in Revelation the eighth and ninth chapters. Then Revelation chapter fifteen and sixteen describes "seven angels having the seven last plagues of God which is the vial judgments which will be poured out upon the earth. Then Jesus will be seen coming from heaven with all his saints to the earth. He [Jesus] will then set up a peaceful kingdom upon the earth.

Here are our plans for the continuing services on Saturday, and Sunday. We will begin teaching the same messages we have taught this past week as we think it is necessary to do so since many of the people haven't been with us in all of the services. There will also be some people who haven't attended at all that attend in the next few weeks. Some of those which have come forward this past week will fall away. They will be the ones which are described in the parable "**The sower and the seed**" as told by Jesus in all three of the synoptic gospel, Matthew, Mark, and Luke. I think we will read the parable to you from Matthew as some of you may not know it.

Here Jesus is interpreting the parable. [Matthew 13:18-23] "Therefore hear the parable of the sower; when anyone hears the word of the kingdom and does not understand it, then the wicked one comes and snatches away what was sown in their heart. This is he who received seed by the **wayside**.

But he who receives seed on **stony places**, this is he who hears the word and immediately receives it with joy; yet he has no root in himself but endures only for awhile. For when tribulation or persecution arises because of the word, immediately he stumbles.

Now he who received seed among the **thorns** is he who hears the word, and the cares of this world and the deceitfulness of riches choke the word and he became unfruitful.

But he who received the seed on **good ground** is he who hears the word and understands it, who indeed bears fruit and produces; some a hundredfold, some sixty, some thirty."

I think we probably have some of those that came forward to receive Christ this past week may fall into any of these three categories. Then there will be those in the fourth category which will stand firm regardless of what may take place in the days to come.

Although for the next 3 or 4 weeks some of you will be hearing the same sermons you have already heard. I beg you to stay with me and attend every service. We will need you to be in prayer for us every service. We ask you to be in prayer through the week as you go to your jobs or what ever you are doing. First pray for yourselves. Satan will try to snatch that which is sown in your heart away, and in the months ahead we all will have persecution. Just remember what Jesus has said, "they persecuted me they will persecute you also." Second pray for those you come in contact with every day, and pray for those who may despitefully use you. Try to be as much like Jesus as you can. Jesus said in [Matthew 5:44] "but I say unto you, love your enemies, bless those who curse you, do good to those who hate you, and pray for those who spitefully use you and persecute you." We may say this is hard to do, and it is. We can only do this if we are close to God, and filled with the Holy Spirit." Next, be sure to pray for Deacon Bill that he will be filled with the Spirit every time he gets up to speak at the stadium. Now does anyone have anything they want to say before we have our closing prayer?

"Yes" said Josie, "Stan and I will be with you every service and we will be praying for you every day."

Others said the same thing.

Deacon Bill said, "If you are going to help us, we would like for you to make your commitment known by coming down front, kneel before the altar and have a united prayer before God. I do not want you to come down unless you really mean business. God said it is better to not make a vow, than to make it and break it. If you are not sure, then you need to pray about it before you commit yourself. We only want those who are committed to God." Many came forward in a committal prayer, but some remained seated.

Pastor R.B. McCartney

The revival continues, others are saved, some fall away because of the cares of life. Stan and Josie continue to work at the hospital, and attend the revival. Bar-Jesus talks more and more about the new credit card and the great society. Brother Lovekin is asking everyone to join the world church; President Dolittle hasn't joined up with the other nations in support of all the things Bar-Jesus is doing. He is afraid it might take away our freedom. Time will tell what will happen next.